Additiona

THE SECRET LANGUAGE *of* TAROT

"The Secret Language of Tarot is the book the tarot world has been waiting for. It's an introduction to the symbols and images of the cards—but it's also a guide to incorporating those symbols in your everyday life. Wald and Ruth Ann Amberstone are two of the world's best tarot teachers. Together, they've developed a comprehensive system for divining the true meanings of the cards. The Amberstones do more than offer a simple list of tarot symbols and definitions; instead, they illuminate the imagery of the cards, and they demonstrate their meaning in the real world. Their work takes symbolism to a whole new level. Read this book, and you'll connect with the cards in ways you couldn't imagine without the Amberstones as your guides. You'll discover new ways to read the tarot. You'll discover new ways to study the cards. And most importantly, you'll discover new ways to refine your own system of thought and analysis. This book will change the way you see the cards—and the world around you."

—CORRINE KENNER,
author of *Tarot Journaling*
and *Simple Fortunetelling with Tarot Cards*

"My first glimpse of this important work came at The Readers Studio, the Amberstone's annual training for Tarot readers, when Wald placed a homegrown early copy of the text in my hands. My heart lept, I breathed a sigh of relief . . . and then I gleefully paid him about 5 times the price of the book we have now. Why? Simple: this book fills a gaping void in esoteric study, and nobody but NOBODY can work this particular magick like the Amberstones. Symbols are the vocabulary of not just Tarot, but of our lives. I've long-dreamed that Wald and Ruth Ann would write this book. It will teach you how to speak in technicolor with yourself and the world."

—ELIZABETH GENCO, writer and Tarotist

"A brilliant and engrossing book that is destined to become a classic. Everyone from the beginning tarot reader to the most experienced psychotherapist can use it to enrich their understanding of symbols. It made me look at tarot imagery with fresh eyes."

—ELINOR GREENBERG, PhD, CGP, CPTR

The SECRET LANGUAGE *of* TAROT

WALD AMBERSTONE &
RUTH ANN AMBERSTONE

WEISER BOOKS
San Francisco, CA / Newburyport, MA

First published in 2008 by
Red Wheel/Weiser, LLC
With offices at:
665 Third Street, Suite 400
San Francisco, CA 94107
www.redwheelweiser.com

Library of Congress Cataloging-in-Publication Data

Amberstone, Wald.
The secret language of tarot / Wald Amberstone and Ruth Ann Amberstone.
p. cm.
ISBN 978-1-57863-416-3 (alk. paper)
1. Tarot. I. Amberstone, Ruth Ann. II. Title.
BF1879.T2A476 2008
133.3'2424—dc22   2007048231

Cover and text design by Sky Peck Design.
Typeset in Hoefler Text.
Cover montage by Kathryn Sky-Peck.

Printed in The United States of America

10 9 8 7 6 5 4 3

For symbol lovers everywhere

CONTENTS

CHAPTER ONE:
CROWNS, PILLARS, THE ROSE AND THE LILY   9

CHAPTER TWO:
PATHS, MOUNTAINS, CROSSES   43

CHAPTER THREE:
MOONS, STARS, POOLS   87

CHAPTER FOUR:
HORSES, SUNS, BANNERS   121

CHAPTER FIVE:
ARMOR, BLINDFOLDS, FEATHERS   157

CHAPTER SIX:

CASTLES, CLOUDS, GARDENS   191

CHAPTER SEVEN:

RIVERS, TOWERS, ANGELS, TEMPLES   219

APPENDIX:

EXERCISES AND SPREADS   271

ACKNOWLEDGMENTS

We offer our love and respect to the many people who have inspired and nurtured the creation of this book: our families, who awakened within us a love of symbolism; our Tarot School students, without whom there would have been no reason to develop this course; Lon Milo DuQuette and Mary K. Greer for their encouragement in presenting this material for publication, their contributions, and for marrying us (not that this was required for our writing projects but it helps!); Holly Voley for providing the scans of the very special deck used to illustrate these pages and for her fascinating background history; David Heizer for his generous and loving technical advice and assistance in preparing the manuscript and illustrations; and Brenda Knight, Amber Guetebier, Jordan Overby, Rachel Leach, Amy Grzybinski, Bonni Hamilton, Anne Hollingworth, and the rest of the staff at Red Wheel/Weiser for welcoming us with such joy and for making this book a reality.

FOREWORD

"The Tarot is symbolism; it speaks no other language
and offers no other signs."

—A. E. WAITE, *The Key to the Tarot*

This statement by A. E. Waite, creator, along with Pamela Colman Smith, of the Rider-Waite-Smith deck used in this book, tells us the single most important thing we need to understand when working with the Tarot. Wald and Ruth Ann Amberstone present an in-depth exploration of twenty-two symbols from this deck, which is the most influential of the last hundred years. But the Amberstones offer more than mere information. This is a course of study involving ways to deepen your understanding and appreciation of how symbols work in this and other decks and in life itself. Studying this book will teach you how to approach any symbol, unfold its potential meanings, and discover, utilizing the deceptively simple exercises and spreads, where and how it is functioning in your life.

This is a practical book. You will learn to use symbols in your readings in several ways:

• Symbols that repeat in more than one card in a spread suggest an important theme in your situation. Several suns, for example, can remind you that life means having the power to act consciously.

• A symbol that jumps out at you and draws your attention has a message for you. When you focus on the horse more than the rider, then it might be urging you to follow your animal instincts.

• A symbol you've never noticed before, once your attention is brought to it through this book, can be key to something that is unnoticed or blocked within yourself but is now ready to be revealed.

• The meanings suggested by the Amberstones can be turned into questions to ask yourself. For instance, by wearing a symbolic blindfold, how or where are you keeping outer world distractions from interfering with deeper insights?

• You will also learn how to find these symbols in yourself by looking within.

But this book is not just a list of correspondences and meanings for the symbols, for what they "signify" turns them into static signs— dead, devoid of energy. But rather, this is a "feeling into" the essence of each symbol—a wonderful circling, spiraling reflection on symbols as dynamic energy signatures on the inner planes, reminders of the truth of being both human and divine. Symbols are what Waite characterized in his book on *The Holy Grail* as "a rumour, a legend, a voice, an unknown witness testifying concerning a more holy . . . and more secret" interiority. He challenged, "Everything depends on the individual mind's capacity to make unto itself a living meaning behind the Symbols and the Sacraments." Your task is to immerse yourself in the presence of this mystery. Following the recommendations in this book will help you do so.

Waite further explained symbolism: "On the highest plane it offers a key to the mysteries." From the Amberstones we learn, for instance, that pillars represent gateways to knowledge and portals both into and out of the secrets or mysteries. Tarot, they explain, is, itself, a temple built of symbols instead of brick or stone, containing within "a glow of the divine presence that can catch fire in you." All these symbols are reminders of some form of truth that is the mystery found at the heart of a temple. To arrive at the heart is realization.

Like Waite, Wald and Ruth Ann Amberstone have dedicated themselves to exploring how Tarot symbols have been designed as "gates which opened on realms of vision beyond occult dreams" (Waite, *Shadows of Life and Thought*). This is what Waite spoke of as the "Secret Tradition," Helena P. Blavatsky as the "Secret Doctrine," and the troubadours as the Holy Grail—long before a watered-down, power-of-mind "Secret" appeared in video format. No, this book will not tell you how to get rich quick. Its secret has to do with the single easiest and the hardest thing there is to do. And it's a secret simply because it can't truly be known until it's experienced, until it's lived.

I welcome you to a book—no, a series of living, breathing seminars—in which you will learn how to approach symbols and make them your own. This is a work that will change and deepen your experience of Tarot forever.

—MARY K. GREER,
author of *Mary K. Greer's 21 Ways to Read a Tarot Card*

ABOUT *the*
CARD ILLUSTRATIONS

In December of 1909 Rider and Son Company released a new Tarot deck by Arthur Edward Waite and Pamela Colman Smith. This deck was done as a commercial project and, according to Waite, "rectified" the Tarot. At that time, Tarots were difficult to acquire in England and had to be imported from the Continent. These imported decks were the then-standard Marseilles type, and the numbered pip cards showed, for example, six cups or eight swords in a pattern. The Waite-Smith deck revolutionized this system by providing scenes on these cards to evoke the meaning of the cards. Now these evocative illustrations are the standard for Tarot decks.

Waite's "rectification" of the deck involved the switching of positions of the Strength and the Justice cards for reasons that he was mysterious about at the time. If you work through the astrological series of signs and their associations with the Majors, you can figure out the answer for yourself.

In the January, 1910, issue of *The Occult Review*, also published by Rider and Son, Ralph Shirley, the editor, mentions that Smith had made a study of fourteenth-century decks prior to illustrating the new deck. This was more than likely done at the instigation of Waite. Waite knew about Tarot. Smith knew about design and illustration. This was a perfect marriage of talents, as the Rider-Waite-Smith (RWS) deck is still in production and still popular, if not the standard for today's decks.

In the same issue, which would have come out in early December (as our magazines come out earlier than their listed month), the deck was offered for sale in several ways—the deck only, described as a "Pack of 78 Tarot Cards" for five shillings, with the cloth book *The Key to the Tarot* in cloth by Waite for seven shillings, six pence, and with a paper version of *The Key* for seven shillings. The book was also available on its own.

The Key to the Tarot, which became *The Pictorial Key* in 1911 when the dimensions of the book increased enough to allow for illustrations, was also a watershed text. Though it is a difficult read at times due to Waite's obfuscations, it gives a solid history of the Tarot and several levels of meanings for the cards, along with several layouts. The best part of this book, which seems to have been reprinted by everyone, is the bibliography. Waite gives scathing reviews of much of the literature available at his time, and it is a good lesson in how to separate fact from fantasy.

Waite, a knowledgeable and prolific writer on occult topics, brought together much of the current thought on Tarot of his day and created something new and dynamic. His ideas for a deck were brilliantly executed by Smith, an artist who never quite achieved enduring success, mostly due to her own failings in business and financial matters. She was adept at book illustration and had a solid grounding in stage design, which is apparent in the deck—each card presents a tableau of meaning that can be deciphered if you know the code. Though the cards for this deck were drawn in less than a year, they show the sophistication and competence of a seasoned artist, who took the requirements of the Tarot structure and created an interpretation that still resonates today.

The deck was reprinted several times, with several changes in the line art as the lithographic plates wore out. For now, there are four versions known called Pam A through Pam D for reference, along with a fifth version—the first printing/first impression Pam A with a blue rose and lilies cardback. This fifth version had a very short and unsuccessful print run. The commonly available deck (from US Games) is from the Pam A line art but has minor changes in coloration due to the difference in printing inks available today. The spirit of the original deck is still present, though some of the subtleties and refinements are missing. The line art from Pam A is also visible in *The Pictorial Key to the Tarot* by Waite.

Many modern decks use the same structure as the RWS, the positions of Strength and Justice notwithstanding. The Minor numbered cards are illustrated, often the same way as in the RWS deck but with a change of clothing and setting. This is not a good thing. The RWS deck has become a template, much as the various European versions of the Marseilles pattern became a template; the illustrations themselves have become the interpretive focus and not the meaning and sense of the card itself. Perhaps someday there will be another blessed collaboration between conception and art as was found in the RWS deck.

I first came across what is now called the Pam A deck in the late '70s at a traveling antique show. The vendor had two decks in boxes, one with a book and one without. I had only limited funds and bought the deck with the book. Why? It was a version of my first and favorite deck, and it was old—the book said it was from 1910. The coloring was also very impressive—the same as my current deck but somehow more subtle and pleasing. This purchase started me on my journey to find out more about the history of the deck and the people involved with it through its many incarnations and reprintings and piracies. It has been a fascinating journey, and though I now know more about the deck and its history, the whole story still eludes me and other researchers. Life should still have mysteries, and this deck is one of them. It is a seminal piece of Tarot history and changed the way we look at the cards. One fine day, another person or persons will reinterpret the Tarot and its imagery and again change our view of it in a global sense. That will be all for the best, as Tarot is a living thing and has changed from a simple gambling game to a divinatory and interpretive tool. Whatever could be next?

These images, from the original printing plates of the Rider-Waite-Smith deck, have been manipulated by Ruth Ann Amberstone to highlight specific details and help focus your attention on the significant details in each card. The more you look at these images, the more you find. This deck has kept me fascinated for more than thirty years. I hope it intrigues you for at least a fraction of that time.

—HOLLY VOLEY
6 March 2007
Bellingham, Washington

INTRODUCTION

If C. G. Jung is right, archetypal images are universal, mysterious, and filled with meaning. If modern tarot theorists are right, tarot is perhaps purely archetypal—its universality, mystery, and meaning contained and expressed entirely by its pictures.

For them, the meanings of the cards, contained in the pictures, are revealed directly and correctly through the workings of the intuition. This would seem to be indisputably true even for completely untutored observers and becomes ever more true with study. People, they say, think primarily in pictures. Pictures make sense and communicate that sense even without the knowledge that comes with study. Have you not found this to be so?

But for those who are fascinated with tarot, untutored intuition is rarely enough. The urge to learn, to study, to know, is irresistible. More than likely, you have experienced this urge yourself.

If you have, and the urge to know is strong in you, you will have discovered that study in tarot is like a grail quest. The grail of tarot is meaning, and it is as elusive as any proper grail must be. The question "What do the cards mean?" is inscribed in invisible ink on the banner of every tarot seeker, including yours.

"What do the cards mean?" is a question that has been answered. It has been answered again and again over the history of the deck. But no answer satisfies completely, and the quest is never done.

If you are one of those who seek meaning in the pictures on the cards, your task has been made both easier and more difficult by the proliferation of decks in modern times. Every tarot deck is distinguished from all others primarily by its pictures, and through its pictures it adds nuance and originality to all that have gone before it. There are thousands of decks, in and out of print, with hundreds more in the works at all times. Perhaps you are working on a deck of your own at this very moment. Hundreds of thousands of pictures have already been painted to provide us with the meanings of seventy-eight mysterious archetypes. Thousands more are on their way. The pleasure and value of diving into this sea of creativity is intense.

But it would seem clear that the grail of meaning has not been captured by this net of pictures, even if there are a million of them. In fact, it seems more elusive than ever, a true likeness lost in a hall of mirrors. This image seems true to me, but I confess that it's only my personal predilection. You must judge for yourself.

It also seems true to me, and for the same reason, that in the end a word may well be worth a thousand pictures. It seems to me that a picture will have no meaning for you unless it is a picture of something with a name you know. And beyond its name, a description and a way to connect it to the rest of what you already know in one way or another.

A picture needs to be of something that can be named, and it needs a description and a context, before it can have meaning.

But once it does, it communicates to us what we know faster than words or even thoughts. To me, this is the value of the pictures of tarot.

That brings us back to the book you are presently holding in your hands. Its value is that it adds a substantial store of knowledge for each picture to translate into meaning and communicate to you at a glance.

The special contribution of this book to the quest for meaning is focus. It narrows the eye's focus and the mind's attention to the separate significant images that compose the picture as a whole. Then each detail of every picture is seen to contain its own treasure of knowledge and to create and transmit its own wealth of meaning. Your intuitive faculty is presented with unimagined wealth on which it can draw with the comfort of a billionaire.

Pictures, even beautiful ones, can't be intriguing or fascinating unless they mean something; tarot pictures are meaningful for you, or it is unlikely that you would have read this far. If you read further, I hope and believe that what you learn will add a great and unexpected depth of pleasure to your own quest for the tarot grail.

A final word, a whisper, to add intensity to your journey. You may well discover, as you travel, that learning suggests doing, and doing can be much more compelling than even the most fascinating knowledge. Enjoy!

—WALD AMBERSTONE
January 1, 2008
New York City

HOW *to* USE *this* BOOK

If you are a tarot reader or a student of the deck, this book was written especially for you. But even if you're not, the fact that you are reading this page makes it likely that you will find its contents fascinating.

Originally written as notes for a course on the imagery of the Rider-Waite-Smith deck, *The Secret Language of Tarot* was created to start you off on an adventure of symbolic inquiry. Even though it can be used as a reference book and enjoyed by dipping into it at random, there's a special benefit that comes from reading it from start to finish. Although each symbol in the book can stand alone, together they lead up to a powerful conclusion.

HOW THE BOOK IS ORGANIZED

Unlike standard symbol dictionaries, *The Secret Language of Tarot* is a course of study and is not organized as an alphabetical listing of symbolic images. Each of the seven chapters contains a set of symbols that share a common theme; the first six chapters contain three symbols each and the seventh chapter contains four, for a total of twenty-two. The concepts that tie each set together may not be obvious at first but will be developed in an integration lesson, which follows each group of symbols. Capping off each chapter is a special symbol spread, created especially for that set.

SIX DIFFERENT WAYS TO USE THIS BOOK

1. Just read it for the pleasure of the exciting and unexpected knowledge it contains. It's a good read for anyone, but especially for tarot people.

2. Use it to strengthen your intuition when doing readings. It contains solid information that will add to your intuitive response to the pictures in the cards. Anyone can look at a tarot card and get a sense of what the card is about in general, but very few actually have any real knowledge of what they're looking at.

3. Use it to translate pictorial symbolism from one deck to another. A crown or a mountain in one deck will carry a very similar connotation in any other deck.

4. Use it as its own divination device, as bibliomancy. Ask a question and open the book to any page for a valid, interesting, and useful answer. It works beautifully!

5. The knowledge and perspective this book contains will increase your enjoyment of the real, everyday world around you. You'll see things like clouds, gardens, pillars, and tall buildings in a very different way, and your appreciation of them will be much enhanced.

6. You may be among the many tarot enthusiasts who are considering creating a new tarot deck of your own. If so, you will find the ideas and detailed information contained in this book immediately helpful as well as suggestive of new and fruitful directions for further research.

Tarot imagery was originally created to evoke an immediate, intuitively sure-footed emotional response from whomever looked at it, whether they knew anything about tarot or not. That is its power and genius. But knowledge is its own reward and produces its own very special and profound pleasure.

Many symbol dictionaries have added to the fund of knowledge about tarot imagery, though the information they contain is often too general, too specialized, or too brief. *The Secret Language of Tarot* was specifically written to add knowledge to your intuitive response to tarot, and also serves to significantly extend what has already been written.

1

CROWNS, PILLARS, THE ROSE *and* THE LILY

Welcome to the Tarot School course on imagery and intuition that we'll call *The Secret Language of Tarot*. In this course, we'll be exploring the meanings of the visual imagery of tarot in considerable detail and in depth. We think that by the time we're done, we'll have created a significant body of work that tarot students will find valuable for research and as important foundation material for the meanings of the cards.

We'll be using the Rider-Waite-Smith imagery as our benchmark, but the information in this course should be transferable to any deck you care to use. We think it will also give your intuition a lot of additional material to work on. The symbolism and significance of the visual imagery of tarot is partly universal, partly esoteric, and partly tarot specific. All of it is historical, and all of it, we hope, will be fun to learn and useful in more ways than one.

CROWNS

We begin with the crowns of tarot. In the RWS deck there are nineteen cards that contain a crown, and these come in many forms, each with a meaning of its own. The nineteen cards are: The High Priestess, The Empress, The Emperor, The Hierophant, The Chariot, Justice, Death, Temperance, The Tower, the Ace of Swords, the 4 of Pentacles, and all the kings and queens.

We'll begin with some meanings for the crown in general, drawn from universal symbolism. The three main aspects of the crown's symbolism are:

1. Being set on the crown (or top) of the head makes it a symbol of overriding significance. It shares the quality of the head (the summit) and what is above the head, a gift from on high. It also sets the seal of transcendence on any great achievement or accomplishment.

2. Its circular shape is a symbol of perfection. It is a ring, worn on the head, that marries what is above to what is below.

3. The material of which a crown is made dedicates the wearer to the form of divinity associated with that material. A gold crown, for example, associates the wearer with the alchemical properties of gold (i.e., purity, perfection, and the attainment of the highest possible states, both inner and outer).

The word "crown" comes from the Latin "corona" and earlier from the Greek "korone" (curved) and "kornu" (horns).

A **corona** is the circle of radiance surrounding a source of illumination. The main physical and symbolic example of a corona is the circle of radiance around the sun. In alchemy, each planet is illustrated as receiving its special radiance in the form of a crown given to it by the sun.

The corona around a physical or symbolic object can be shown as a concentric circle or as emanating rays. A halo, for example, is a spiritual corona surrounding the head of a spiritually elevated being.

A **diadem** is a crown in the form of a circlet around the head or around the ceremonial hat on the head of a royal figure. It is a symbol of a divinely supported secular authority.

A **glory** is an arc or a circle of rays around another visual symbol, suggesting divine inspiration or protection.

Korone, the Greek word for curved, is used in this context for any form of circle or circlet worn on the head to signify a connection with the gods. This includes the wreath, the crest, and horns, as well as the crown, diadem, and tiara.

Examples of different kinds of crowns in tarot include the:

- horns of Isis (The High Priestess)
- diadem of the zodiac (The Empress)
- domed crown (The Emperor, The Tower)
- papal tiara (The Hierophant)
- celestial diadem (The Chariot)
- toothed crown (Justice, the 4 of Pentacles)
- glory (Temperance)
- stylized diadems (kings and queens)

The crown in all times and places has been associated with royalty, and royalty is conferred only by the divine recognition, symbolized by the crown. The crown is also a symbol of ultimate achievement, the sign of victory and pre-eminence in any field of endeavor (e.g., a crowning achievement, a heavyweight-boxing crown). In organisms, the crown is the top, as in the crown of the head or the crown of a tree.

No one can become the king or the queen of a kingdom of any kind without a crown. A coronation, the ritual of establishing legitimate royal authority, is the ritual of placing a crown on someone's head.

Each separate crown in tarot has its own symbolism. Here are three examples:

The High Priestess

The crown of The High Priestess is the crown of Isis/Hathor, two names of the Egyptian self-created Great Mother Goddess who brought forth everything else. Hathor was the Queen of Heaven, and Isis was the "Oldest of the Old who existed from the beginning."

In both forms, as Isis and as Hathor, the goddess is said to have given birth to the sun. Hathor was the Nile Goose who laid the golden egg of the sun, and Isis was the womb of Horus who was the reincarnation of Osiris. The womb enclosing Horus in hieroglyphics is "Hat—Hor" or Hathor.

Isis and Hathor as a pair were sometimes known as the Bright Mother and the Dark

Mother. In later times, Isis was paired with her dark twin sister, Nepthys. Together they guaranteed the immortality of the pharaohs in the form of birth, death, and resurrection.

The visual emblem of these paired goddesses, as illustrated by the crown of The High Priestess, was the sun disk lying between the horns of the Moon-Cow Goddess. The central sun disk signifies the male spirit soon to be reborn (Horus), enclosed and protected by the horns of the goddess, one light and one dark.

In Hellenistic and Roman culture, Isis was highly revered as the Divine Mother, "eternal savior of the race of men." The image of Isis suckling Horus became the model for images of the Virgin Mary holding the infant Jesus. Parts of the myth and worship of Isis were transferred to Mary early in the Christian era.

The crown of Isis combines in The High Priestess with her watery robes and the sickle moon at her feet, symbols of Mary as Stella Maris (Star of the Sea), to join primary Egyptian and Christian spirituality in a single Hermetic image.

Also, the lunar symbolism of The High Priestess's crown (waxing, full, and waning phases of the moon) is revered in Neo-Paganism as the special sign of the Triple Goddess (Maiden, Mother, Crone).

All together, the crown of The High Priestess is a universal symbol of the original authority of the divine feminine. In a reading, it will be useful to remember the power of all things feminine, the moon and its phases, and women's spirituality.

The Hierophant

The crown of The Hierophant is a three-tiered, toothed golden crown—three gold diadems signifying divinely sanctioned rule over three kingdoms. The segmented, or toothed, top of a crown is a symbol of rays of the sun's light.

The papal tiara is a triple diadem over a simple cap called a *camelaucum* from the Byzantine court of the seventh and eighth centuries, where it was a sign of high social status. The diadems were added one at a time over several hundred years and probably are more ornamental than symbolic. Still, the papal tiara signifies both a spiritual and a secular authority—rule over the Catholic Church and over the territory of the Vatican.

Simultaneously, it is a Masonic reference hidden in a Christian one. The three tiers of the crown refer to the three degrees of Masonry, the three levels of initiation, and the three levels of attainable human consciousness. It is the symbol of the Teacher.

The lowest level is the first degree of Entered Apprentice, whose field of endeavor is his physical body and his social existence. The Entered Apprentice strives to perfect his physical habits, his work ethic, and his social behavior.

The second level corresponds to the second degree of Fellowcraft, or Masonic journeyman, whose field of endeavor is his mind and his psyche. This involves self-examination and psychological healing and wholeness, as well as academic study and intellectual refinement.

The third level is that of a Master Mason, whose work is spiritual. His concern is the heart and the soul, both his own and others'. As compassion, this concern takes the form of teaching and moral and symbolic leadership.

The gold color of the crown is an alchemical reference to purity and the perfection of the self in the Great Work.

The three vertical lines at the top of the crown are a Qabalistic reference to the Hebrew letter associated with The Hierophant, which is Vav. It means "hook" and refers to the manner in which The Hierophant, as the great teacher of tarot, binds together the highest of teachings with the physicality of his disciples.

In a reading, The Hierophant's crown should remind you of spiritual leadership, moral, psychological and spiritual effort, and the learning process in general.

The Chariot

The crown of The Chariot is a Masonic symbol, a composite of sun, moon, and stars and glory. This is one form of the Masonic Rule of Three, which generally states that every visible thing is paired, made of an active and a passive, an exuberant and a severe, a bright and a pale, a stable and a changeable aspect, and that an invisible divine moderating principal binds the opposites together.

The sun is the symbol of everything active, exuberant, bright, and stable. The moon and stars are the symbol of what is passive, severe, pale, and changeable. The glory is the symbol of the divine perspective, which sees itself in every manifested form and resolves all dualities. In this card, the crown is a visual symbol of the consciousness that seeks to rule itself by bringing all forms of inner opposition into harmony. The sun, moon, and stars and glory represent all inner forms and forces harnessed to a single will and a central wisdom.

The crown is also a Qabalistic reference to the card's esoteric title, The House of Influence, which brings all good things from above to below and from below to above. It is a spiritualized astrology of sun, moon, and stars and a ruling, organizing, encompassing glory, the invisible whole that is hidden in its visible parts.

In a reading, the crown of The Chariot reminds you of balance, harmony, self-control, and the wisdom to pull opposing forces together. It can also be a reminder of the blessings that flow from such harmony.

PILLARS

The people who created the system of imagery in the Rider-Waite-Smith deck were pretty serious people. Not much of a sense of humor, very much in their heads, not much heart, we think. But their thinking and their pictures are actually very interesting in themselves.

We're at the beginning of a course on the meaning of tarot imagery, and you might have a question that ought to be answered. That question is, "What does this information do for me?" It is esotericism, art history, symbolism in general—maybe it's interesting, maybe not, but is it connected to you in some way? How might it be personal?

Well, here's how. The whole deck is a special construction of symbols, and they have only two purposes here:

1. They show you a path to your own highest nature, what is best and purest in you. They point to the path of return for anyone who wants to travel it. This may or may not be important

to you now, but at some time in your life, you may find yourself very happy to have those pointers.

2. They bring divine energy down to the level of the everyday world, where they talk about everyday things in a powerful and useful way and teach you how to do the same.

In both directions they remind you of tarot's version of how the world is made and how a human being is made, so you can use tarot to help yourself and others. It's hard to be a doctor if you don't know anatomy, and meaningful images are the anatomy of tarot.

Symbols act something like electrical transformers. When electricity is generated at the power plant, it's measured in thousands and tens of thousands of volts. When you use electrical current to power your home appliances, you can use only 110 volts at a time. Between the source and its ultimate uses stands a whole series of what are called step-down transformers, which make something overwhelming into something convenient and useful. In tarot, the visual imagery serves this function.

In the previous section we talked about the crown. What is important to remember about a crown is that if you are ever entitled to wear one, it makes you unique. In any kingdom there is only one true crown, and it is the symbol of what is best, highest, and most responsible in the wearer.

At its best, the crown marries the wearer to his or her highest self. At its worst, it gives authority to someone who hasn't earned it, creating a tyrant.

And now we come to the pillar.

What you most need to know and remember about the pillar in general is its masculinity. It rises vertically from the horizontal plane of the earth. It is intended to be an absolute contrast to things as they normally are. It is a symbol of intentional difference. Of course, there are times when the pillar becomes feminine, but we'll get to that later.

Pillars serve four main purposes:

1. to support
2. to define
3. to identify
4. to separate

In its function as support, a pillar keeps what is raised up from coming down. This is true in a building, where structural pillars hold up roofs and upper stories. To damage or remove such a pillar threatens the entire structure. This is also true in social and symbolic structures. Certain traditions, rites, and individuals are considered pillars whose presence supports the whole structure. Even heaven is supposed to be supported by pillars.

The function of support implies will, endurance, purpose, and the ability to surrender individuality to the common good. The pillar here is a humble servant.

The second function of a pillar is definition. In this form, strength is not the issue and a single pillar is not enough. It must be one of many, whose purpose is to create a line or circle on one side of which is the ordinary everyday world and on the other is a special, even a consecrated space. Here, too, the individuality implied in the phallic vertical shaft is subordinated to the higher purpose of the group.

The third function is to serve as a proud marker for the existence of a god or a hero. When such a pillar is erected, it is a statement: "Here dwells the spirit of . . . , whose name is sacred or glorious." In this form only, a pillar stands alone, supporting nothing but an important memory or serving as a living reminder of some potent personality.

None of these three functions can be found in the RWS tarot. So why mention them? Just for the fun of it, or in case you come across pillars serving these functions in other decks.

The fourth function of a pillar is to separate one condition from another. This function uses pillars in pairs, as a gateway or entrance to sacred space and the mysteries of a higher condition or consciousness. This is how the pillar appears in tarot, on just three cards: The High Priestess, The Hierophant, and Justice.

Let me remind you here that tarot is nothing but a concoction whipped up out of symbols. The RWS deck in particular is a world of symbols with a lineage. And this lineage has three levels:

1. The ritual universe of the Order of the Golden Dawn. Many of its symbols were drawn into tarot, and tarot itself is used in its rituals. It is a universal language that can translate one kind of magical jargon into another. In tarot, alchemy easily becomes Qabalah, which becomes astrology and numerology, and so on.

2. The Golden Dawn, in turn, drew heavily on the symbolism and ritual of Freemasonry, which has no dealings with tarot at all. The Waite deck gets its symbolism from Freemasonry more than any other source.

3. Masonic symbolism emerges from a mix of biblical, Greek, and Egyptian philosophy and religion, each of which tried in its own way to explain God, man, and the world. Freemasonry turned these explanations into galleries of images and pictures that it mixed and merged in its own way to make its own explanation of the nature of things.

So this brings us back to pillars and tarot. There are, as we said, just three cards in our deck that have pillars on them, The High

Priestess, The Hierophant, and Justice. If you understand the pillars of The High Priestess, you understand the essence of the others. And here the pillars become feminine.

The High Priestess

There are three visual aspects of the pillars of The High Priestess that especially stand out:

First, the pillars of The High Priestess are a pair—so you know you're looking at a symbol of initiation. On one side of the gateway they create is the person who is looking at them—mainly you, out in the world, ignorant, but knowing that important knowledge awaits when you pass between them. The pillars are considered to be the labia that mark the vaginal entrance to the Holy of Holies, the location of the feminine mysteries.

Second, one pillar is black and one is white. You would naturally tend to believe that this is the symbolism of complementary opposites, like night and day, darkness and light. In this you would be correct. Ceremonial Magick appears to have introduced these colors in its own version of Egyptian ritual, but I haven't seen any evidence that this is actually Egyptian.

In a popular form of an esoteric initiation ceremony there is a version of the Egyptian Hall of Truth where the black and white pillars stand at the entrance. The candidate for initiation is brought before these pillars and there makes a "negative confession." The individual states that he or she is not guilty of a particular list of sins and failings associated with forty-two judges who reside within the Hall. The candidate must demonstrate specific esoteric knowledge and declare several levels of purification, in addition to the negative confession, before being allowed to go further. All these procedures are incised as decoration on the two pillars, although that is not shown on the card.

The third and most mysterious feature is the letter on each pillar. A white B appears on the black pillar and a black J appears on the white pillar. These letters stand for Boaz and Jachin, respectively, which were the names given to the two pillars that stood before Solomon's Temple. We're sure of that from direct biblical quotes. After that, nothing is certain. There is no written biblical or Talmudic explanation for these names, and all the esoteric explanations are guesswork or invention.

The standard translation of "Boaz" is "in him is strength," but it needs to be understood that this strength is in him as potential, the way a child is in the womb waiting to be born. It isn't there yet. And "Jachin," which is usually translated as "God establishes," is more accurately "God prepares," and the biblical commentary says that this refers to the coming of the Messiah. Nowhere in biblical commentary are the two names connected in any way. Although there certainly must be some connection, it was never written down. This is one example of a biblical secret that remains strictly oral.

An interesting note is that in some Masonic literature, "Jachin" becomes "Joachim." And Joachim was the father of the Joseph, who married Mary, who gave birth to Jesus.

What the names on the pillars do is connect Egyptian with biblical tradition. They bring into the picture the symbolism of Solomon's Temple, which is extremely important to both the Western esoteric tradition in general and to Masonic tradition in particular. The Solomonic pillars, by the way, were not black and white but brass. Also, a biblical verse refers to an ornamentation of pomegranates around the tops of both pillars. Since there was no room to picture this ornamentation on the pillars in the card, they were transferred to the veil between the pillars.

All the final secrets of Western magic as a spiritual path are said to be located in the Temple behind the pillars. The pillars are the only approach to these secrets, and Freemasonry considers itself to be that entranceway, to be the very pillars themselves.

Justice

The pillars of Justice describe the part of an initiation ritual in which the candidate stands between the pillars, under the Balance of Justice, and names and explains the significance of all of the pillars' parts. This is a test the candidate must not fail but for which he or she has carefully prepared, since the information is fairly elaborate. In the card of Justice, the pillars are pictured as plain, so as not to give away the answers to the test.

The Hierophant

In The Hierophant, the pillars with the Hierophant between them are the ritual symbol of Osiris on his throne, the Egyptian deity presiding over the entire process of initiation.

Because we don't have a lot of space, and because it doesn't serve our specific purpose, we won't go into the symbolism of the pillars' construction or other aspects of ritual. What you want to remember here is that the pillars are the place and also the effort of initiation. All the secrets that become the universe pass between these pillars into the world, and everyone who wants to know these secrets has to come to these pillars and find a way to pass between them.

I think most of you know that the primary energy of tarot is understood to be sexual energy. Well, here's sexual energy as the lust for knowledge.

The pillars are symbols of all the gateways to new and important knowledge in our lives, to the improvement of our lives through knowledge, and of the importance of making the effort to learn.

THE ROSE AND THE LILY

Welcome to our class on the symbol of the rose and the lily. Now, the rose is a symbol by itself. So is the lily. But the rose and the lily is a compound symbol that is different than either of its constituent parts.

The rose appears, in red and in white, by itself in many cards. But the lily never appears alone. Wherever you find a lily in the RWS deck, you find a red rose.

There are just five cards that contain this symbol: two Majors, two Minors, and a court card. The Majors are The Magician and The Hierophant; the Minors are the Ace of Pentacles and the 2 of Wands. The court card is the King of Pentacles. In this class, we'll be talking about the first four of these. The King of Pentacles will have a place of honor all by himself in the next class. As you may have come to expect, our symbol means different things in different cards. But before we talk about these.cards, let's look at the two flowers as separate symbols.

The Lily

The lily, in olden times, was the floral emblem of several goddesses. One was the northern European goddess Eostre. Her name was derived from the ancient word for spring: "eastre." This goddess is the source of both the name of the holiday of Easter and its association with the lily.

Juno, the Roman equivalent of the Greek goddess Hera, is also associated with the lily. Roman Pagans said that the first lily sprang from her breast milk. Roman Christians said that the lily sprang from the breast milk of Mary.

In Europe, the lily became the symbol of the female "cup" containing the essence of life. The word "chalice" derives from "calyx," the word referring to the cup of the lily flower. The lily is a symbol of the miraculous impregnation of virgin goddesses. According to Roman mythology, the "blessed virgin Juno" gave birth to the god Mars by means of an immaculate conception. The parallel with Mary and Jesus is obvious.

Lilies are synonymous with whiteness, therefore with purity, innocence, and virginity. But because of its spicy-sweet scent, the lily has been characterized by some as an aphrodisiac and associated with Venus and the satyrs. Because of its prominent phallic pistils, the lily is also perceived as masculine. This combination of qualities is said to be one of the reasons why the kings of France chose the lily (*fleur de lis*) as the emblem of French royalty.

Because of its whiteness, the lily has been described as lunar, pale, and connected to silver, a symbol of love unfulfilled and/or sublimated. As pure, sublimated love, the lily is a symbol of Christ.

In the Song of Solomon, there is a famous line that reads: "As the lily among the thorns, so is my love among the daughters." It is a reference to Israel's position among the nations and Mary's position among women.

The famous line from the Gospel of Matthew reads, "Consider the lilies of the field, how they grow. They toil not, nor do they spin." By placing themselves in the hands of divine providence, lilies prosper. The lily thus becomes a symbol of surrender to divine grace.

In a famous early Christian sermon, the lily of the valley is likened to Christ (the lily) in the world of men (the valley)—the redeemer in the midst of sin, purity in the midst of impurity.

The lily has six petals, and in esoteric lore it is a symbol of the cool and distant macrocosm, the world above in the axiom, "As above, so below."

The Rose

The rose, on the other hand, has five petals (the original, not the genetically bred varieties). It is the symbol of the heat of passion and involvement, the microcosm, the world below.

But the rose, too, is dual in its sexual symbolism. It is, first of all, the emblem of Venus, goddess of love and passion. And from this primary attribution comes the story of how the rose became a symbol of secrecy and confidentiality.

Rome adopted the Egyptian sun god Horus as part of the cult of Isis that came to them through Greece. The Greeks had taken him over as Horus the child. His name in Egyptian was *her-pa-khrad*, and the Greeks turned it into Harpocrates. The hieroglyph for a child was a seated boy sucking his finger. The Greeks thought this showed him with his finger to his lips, and so they made him the god of silence and secrecy.

The cult of Harpocrates became very popular especially among upper-class Romans. There is a famous story from those times in which Cupid was said to have given a rose to Harpocrates as a thank-you gift for not telling tales about his mother Venus, the goddess of sensual love. So the rose became the symbol of confidentiality in the classical Roman world. The ceilings of dining rooms were decorated with roses to remind guests that what was said there when they were drunk was *sub rosa* (under the rose) and was therefore privileged and not to be made public. The phrase "sub rosa" and its meaning was well known and used all throughout Europe from Roman times to the present day. It even appeared as a symbol in the confessional.

From the carnality of Venus, the rose passes to the purity of Mary, as the sign of her love, compassion, and perfection. And from there it becomes the emblem of alchemical perfection, symbol of the Sun.

But in another form of Christian symbolism, the rose takes on a masculine character. It becomes the emblem of Christ, of the blood of his sacrifice—the token of his love and compassion for humanity. Thus the rose becomes the sign of the Rosicrucians, the Order of the Rose Cross, whose primary symbol and core mystical perception is the vision of the rose emanating from the point of juncture of the arms of the cross.

The single five-petaled red rose is a general sign of completion and perfection. Specifically it is a symbol of:

- the mystic center (as in the Rose Cross)
- the heart (as in the Sacred Heart of Mary and Jesus)
- the Garden of Eros (of Venus and Cupid)
- the Beloved (in the Song of Solomon)

The white rose is a symbol of rebirth and immortality.
The gold rose is a symbol of consummate achievement.
The blue rose is a symbol of the impossible.
The five-petaled rose is a circular mandala of the esoteric conception of microcosm. The seven-petaled rose corresponds to all things seven, such as the seven directions, the seven traditional planets, and the seven alchemical metals. The eight-petaled rose is a symbol of regeneration similar to the white rose.

• • •

Now the time has come to talk about the four cards in which the rose and the lily appear together as a single compound symbol.

The Magician

In the landscape of The Magician, red roses hang in garlands from the top of the card above The Magician's head. The top of his double-tipped wand points directly at the roses above him. There are also a number of roses at the bottom of the card. The lilies can be found only at the bottom of the card, where they are large and distinct.

Here, the rose and the lily refer mainly to the esoteric function of The Magician, which is the double function of life and death. He brings things to life by paying attention to them and allows them to die by ignoring them.

Part of the symbolism of the rose is the heat and passion of life. Roses are the traditional flowers of betrothals, weddings, and declarations of love. Roses are edible and are an ingredient in magickal, culinary, and healing herbal ingestibles. Lilies, especially the lily of the valley, are funeral flowers. They are poisonous and associated with death, but they are also associated with purity and redemption, which are religious funerary themes.

In the picture on the card, the blood red flowering rose is a symbol of the feminine path of emergence, of embodiment in life. The white, trumpet-shaped lily, with its prominent phallic pistils, is a symbol of the masculine path of return to the world of spirit. Although it can be disturbing to realize, the path of return is a journey to disembodiment and at least a spiritual death. Sometimes this journey can involve martyrdom and actual death in the service of a divinity.

The rose and the lily in tarot are the symbols of the Qabalistic drop of red and drop of white that create the world in all its bewildering multiplicity. Simultaneously, they are the alchemical red and white, whose marriage is a token of ultimate unity and the resolution of all disharmonies.

These two themes of creating and dissolving the complexities of existence are the life and death functions of The Magician, and the symbol of the rose and the lily illustrates both themes equally and simultaneously.

In a practical application of this idea, if The Magician comes up in a reading, you could say that positive things come alive for you when you pay attention to them and work at them. But they wither and perish if you ignore them long enough. On the other hand, you could say that you aggravate and energize a difficult situation by obsessing about it, but you can purify and heal negativity by denying it importance and attention.

The Hierophant

Here, the rose and the lily appear as the distinguishing marks of two kinds or styles of learning. Two acolytes kneel before The Hierophant, each imbibing his teachings in a completely different way, each leading down a different path to the same goal.

The rose is a symbol of the path of the heart, of devotion and love. On this path, a seeker surrenders his or her heart to the loving compassion of the teacher and the beauty of the path as it is revealed. It is said that the only language of the heart is tears, and when you are filled with love, all you can do is let your tears well up and cry. The rose is a symbol of unconditional love, such as the love between mother and child and the love between a great being and his or her disciples. To learn what The Hierophant has to teach, love and devotion are all that is needed.

The lily is the path of the mind, of purity, renunciation, and knowledge. On this path, a seeker becomes ascetic. Through the effort of resisting the temptations of a passionate nature and through endless study, you can raise and purify any desire, intention, or path and in the end reach the lofty goals set by an elevated teaching.

The choice between these two approaches to morality, ethics, wisdom, and spiritual leadership is dictated by personal predilection. Some take one path, some the other.

The issues here often involve moral or ethical choices and how to approach them. What is separated by the rose and the lily is joined and resolved by The Hierophant. Issues of tolerance and a need for discrimination versus conviction and a need to make hard choices arise when The Hierophant turns up and your attention is drawn to the rose and the lily.

2 of Wands

The first Minor Arcana card with the rose and the lily in it is the 2 of Wands. In this card, the compound symbol of these two flowers as a visual unit is the clearest of all. On a gray stone block that is part of the castle's parapet and that has the approximate proportions of a double cube altar (another symbol for another time), there is a white square. In the white square is a tilted equal-armed cross. Each arm of the cross is a living plant stem, and on the ends of each of the four arms is a blossom. These blossoms are alternating roses and lilies.

So what could this be about? At first glance, there are alchemical and Rosicrucian possibilities here. But neither of these has any particular relevance to the 2 of Wands and wouldn't have a prominent place on this card.

We had spoken earlier of how the lily has a mythical connection with Juno, the mother of Mars, whose color is the red of the rose. That only has a passing connection with this card through its astrological attribution of Mars in Aries. But it is the astrological attribution that turns out to be important. This will take a moment to explain.

Each of the Minor Arcana cards (except the aces) has an astrological attribution consisting of a planet in a sign. If you work with just the 2 through 10, that gives you nine cards in each of the four suits, or thirty-six cards. Each card therefore equals 10 degrees of a circle, or a decan. The thirty-six decans equal the 360 degrees of a complete circle. Each decan contains either ten or eleven days to make the 365 days of the year. That works neatly. Three cards, or 30 degrees, make one astrological sign, and the twelve signs of the zodiac make the complete wheel of the year.

Well, the 2 of Wands is Mars in Aries, which is the beginning of spring. This is the start of the warm part of the year after winter has come to an end, and it is symbolized in this card by Mars as the rose.

Now comes the astrological rub that gives us the lily part of the symbol.

In the ancient astronomy used in tarot, only seven planets existed. because that was all that could be seen with the naked eye. So up to the beginning of the twentieth century, when the most distant planets were discovered, astrology used only those planets.

That meant that there were seven planets to assign to the thirty-six decans that make up a year. Seven, as you can see, doesn't divide evenly into thirty-six. When you divide thirty-six by seven, you get five, with one left over. So one planet had to appear six times instead of five. Mars was chosen to be that planet, and it appears for the second time in the 10 of Cups as Mars in Pisces, the end of winter. Pisces is the last sign of winter, just as Aries is the beginning of spring. The esoteric community decided that an extra boost of energy was needed to make the transition from winter's cold to spring's warmth, and Mars was chosen to be the planetary symbol of that energy. So Mars in Pisces is followed by Mars in Aries. The lily, associated with the alchemical cold of a water sign, is followed by the rose, associated with the alchemical heat of a fire sign. This order of water sign followed by fire sign, cold followed by heat, is repeated throughout the zodiac.

In this symbol, mythology, astrology, and alchemy are joined together. The issues here are an ending leading to a new beginning, the conclusion of one cycle with all its drama and the beginning of a completely new story, something already achieved and something waiting to be done—all accomplished with the warlike intensity of Mars. This is one implication of the esoteric title of the 2 of Wands, the Lord of Dominion.

Ace of Pentacles

The final landscape featuring the rose and the lily is the Ace of Pentacles.

Here the meaning is simple. The lily assumes pride of place, being in the foreground of the card, and roses are smaller, less distinct, and in the background of the card. In part, the picture shows a well-kept garden, with short green grass in the midst of which cultivated lilies grow on long stalks. Far away, mountain peaks can be seen through the arched opening in a hedge, which separates the garden from the distant heights. Roses grow small and wild in the greenery of the hedge.

The meaning of rose and lily is a biblical reference to a famous line from the Song of Solomon, which says, "I am the lily of the valley and the rose of the deep." In Qabalistic lore, the rose in this case is associated with grace and the lily with judgment, and both flowers are to be found in Malkuth, the bottom of the Tree of Life and the end of the journey of emergence. Malkuth is the valley and the deep, symbolized in the Ace of Pentacles by the garden and the hedge respectively.

In Christian symbolism, Christ is referred to as the lily who dwells in the valley, a symbol of the promise of redemption in the midst of a mundane existence.

Here the issue is the acceptability of an unfettered joy in the real world just as it appears. Is it OK to enjoy life without hesitation or any need of repentance? Is the world OK without fixing? Is creation good as it stands? Or do pain and suffering require us to turn to spirituality for solace and explanation? Is the world of the flesh inherently evil? Once again, each person will be drawn by his or her personal style more to one approach than the other.

• • •

In all the differences of interpretation in these four cards, the rose and the lily together describe the underlying primal mystery of male and female, of the sexual energy from which the universe descended and by means of which it will return to its original purity and wholeness.

For alchemy, the Great Work of separating the fine from the gross, of raising the high from the low, and achieving sublime perfection is symbolized by the Alchemical Wedding of sun and moon, rose and lily, red and white. In their union, everything is completed and humanity returns to divinity the original gift of perfection.

In a Kabbalistic midrash a comparison is made between God and an artist. An artist, they say, creates a great painting, and the painting is applauded. But God creates the whole universe, and the universe praises its creator. When an artist creates a great painting, the painting endures but the artist perishes. When God creates the universe, God endures and the universe passes. An artist creates his painting with a palette of many colors. But God creates the entire universe with a drop of red and a drop of white.

The rose and the lily are that drop of red and drop of white. Their combined beauties are the underlying beauty of the whole of creation, and their mingled fragrance is the incense of divinity that pervades every force and form, every name and change, that makes the universe.

The power of the rose and the lily is to beget love. When you fall in love, it is the beauty of the rose and lily you see in your beloved. When you discover wisdom and experience devotion, it is the fragrance of the rose and lily that fills the sacred chalice you have become.

INTEGRATION: CROWNS, PILLARS, THE ROSE AND THE LILY

Most of the images in tarot, even the little bits and pieces of larger pictures, are symbols, and all symbols are reminders of some form of truth. Every symbol in the deck has a spiritual, intellectual, emotional, and practical aspect, and every one is useful at one time or another.

Here are some of the issues that arise from the imagery of crowns, pillars, and the rose and lily. The issues are not definitive. Instead, they are meant to provoke thought, feeling, and discussion.

Crowns

When a crown catches your attention in a reading, you can be sure it concerns a matter of overriding importance.

A crown is always a gift from above—sometimes in recognition of a great achievement, sometimes as a demand for such an achievement.

Crowns require their wearers to be perfect. They recognize the potential in a person for such perfection, and accepting a crown is an acknowledgement of the demand for perfection.

The energy of a crown is a source of light, illumination, and radiance. One who wears a crown is expected to be such a source of illumination of others.

The outward authority conferred by a crown begins with an inner authority. And with authority comes responsibility.

There are visible and invisible crowns, acknowledged and unacknowledged authority. Whoever wears a crown is the source of power and legitimacy. There are hidden teachers, exiled royalty, lineages of master and disciple where a crown passes in secret from an older to a younger head.

Each crown is special and confers its own authority and responsibility. A particular crown gives you a particular job—to protect, to teach, to lead, to reconcile, to save.

A crown is most of all a ring, signifying the marriage of the giver and the wearer. It is the commitment of the giver to empower, protect, and love the wearer. It is the reciprocal commitment of the wearer to perform to the utmost the duties that come with the crown, to surrender to the love of the giver, and above all, to return that love completely. This is equally true of a spouse and a king.

Pillars

By itself, a single pillar is masculine. By itself, a pillar can be a humble support that carries the weight of a whole structure. Your spinal column is masculine, and it supports your whole being. But you pay no attention to it unless it hurts.

By itself, a pillar can get your attention. Its uprightness and visibility lend pride, honor, and recognition to a person or event worth remembering.

In combination, pillars are feminine. In rows or circles, pillars define sacred and special places. Together they make an inside and an outside.

The outside is reserved for the ordinary and governed by the laws of the lowest common denominator. The outside is the place of the many, the place for everyday concerns governed by custom, necessity, and universally accepted social standards.

The inside is the place of the unusual, the hidden, and the secret. Different rules apply here, and only those who need and deserve to know those rules know them. The inside demands the highest, best, purest, and most powerful qualities. It is the place of the few, forbidden to the many.

The outside and the inside negate each other, but need each other. Each is the justification for the other.

In pairs, pillars are also the gateway from outside to inside. They are the means of passage. Each pillar in a pair is half of what is necessary to gain entrance to the hidden, the special, and the sacred. Each is half of an argument, half of an irreconcilable difference. By means of either half alone, no passage is possible, no entrance is granted. One side of an argument, one position out of two, leads to nowhere but itself.

A pair of pillars presents a challenge and an imperative. You can't pass to the secrets and wonders within unless you meet the challenge and resolve it. You can't ignore the challenge either. You only become aware of it because it is important to you, perhaps even crucial. If you turn away, you will have been defeated without even trying. And such a defeat causes pervasive sadness and permanent regret.

To accept the challenge is a masculine response to the lure of a feminine treasure. And it carries risks. First is the risk of failure.

Second is the risk of success. And third is the risk of involvement and commitment. To meet the challenge and pass through the gateway of the pillars is to find out who you always were but never knew, to gain the totality of yourself. This is the inner nature of initiation.

On the outside of the gateway you are a civilian. On the inside, you are who you were meant to be. The more imposing the pillars, the more difficult the passage and the greater the person awaiting you on the other side.

The Rose and the Lily

Each by itself is wonderful and opposite. The rose is passionate, involved, understanding, and intimate. These qualities give the greatest pleasure, make the experience of life intense, and are great companions in good times and bad. The lily is pure, dispassionate, wise, and distant. As qualities, these make excellent advisors in the midst of confusion, trusted friends and reliable supports in times of crisis, and they offer solutions when things get impossible.

Together they create beauty, love, desire, and the goodness in everything. A vision of the rose and the lily annihilates ugliness and falsehood. A whiff of their scent carries you through pain and sorrow.

They offer the gifts of a great life and a good death. They are the secret powers of pointing to and turning away.

Together they are in love, not at war. Rose and lily, heart and mind, allow each other completion. Each is enough by itself. Each makes the other a complete path to any goal.

In sequence, their energy brings one chapter of a story to a close and opens the next. Winter finds the energy to become spring.

They teach you to enjoy this world, to become perfect in it, to rise above it, and to find the secret center of yourself.

SYMBOL SPREAD:
THE TWO PILLARS, THE ROSE, THE LILY,
AND THE CROWN

This is the first in a series of spreads based upon the tarot symbols studied in this course. It makes use of the concepts discussed in the classes on the pillars, the rose and lily, and the crown, and it is ideally suited for conflict resolution readings.

The layout below consists of two vertical columns of four cards each—the Pillars—spaced about six inches apart. The left-hand pillar represents one side of the conflict—a person, group, choice, or idea. The right-hand pillar represents the opposing side.

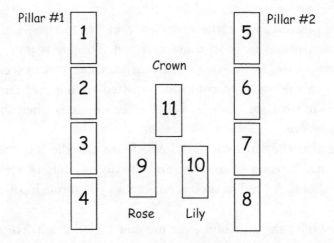

Three inches or so up from the bottom, two cards are placed in the central area between the pillars. The card on the left is the Rose. The card on the right is the Lily. They are separated from each other by the space of one card.

Directly above that space, place the final card—the Crown.

Each four-card Pillar describes the energies and characteristics that make up that side of the conflict. They point out the core issues that are important to that side—those things that define its position in the conflict and that are holding it back from reaching resolution. Although read sequentially, each set of four cards should be considered as a group.

Each card in a Pillar should be contrasted with the card in the same position in the opposite Pillar. So you have four sets of pairs: 1–5, 2–6, 3–7, and 4–8. For example, let's say card #1 is The Magician and card #5 is The Star reversed. On the one hand, the first pillar is expressing a focused and willful energy, while the card opposite it might indicate a lack of equilibrium and a sense that all is not right with the world. Perhaps there might be a wish for quiet withdrawal as opposed to going full steam ahead. You can see right away how these opposing energies can contribute to the conflict.

The three cards in the center hold the key to how the two sides can work towards passing between the pillars and moving forward together.

The Rose is the path of the heart. The card in this position will show the nature of a loving way to proceed—how to express emotions in a positive way.

The Lily is the path of the mind. The card in this position will show the nature of a rational way to proceed—what to focus mental energy on.

The Crown defines the higher purpose of the conflict and its resolution and is the outcome to hold as a common goal.

Although much can be seen from this spread in a quick read, we suggest you leave the cards out for a while (or write them in a notebook) and contemplate them over a period of time. Conflicts made up of the immovable blocks that make up the pillars are usually not resolved overnight and bear thoughtful consideration and persistent effort.

May this spread help find a way through for you and for those who seek your guidance.

2

PATHS,
MOUNTAINS, CROSSES

PATHS

Welcome to our class on the image of the path in tarot, which occurs in four cards—the 8 of Pentacles, the Ace of Pentacles, The Moon, and Temperance.

As you know, we've already done a number of classes on the meaning of imagery in the Rider-Waite-Smith deck. To make classes like that happen, we have to do quite a bit of research, and up to now it's been fairly easy. But our experience this time was different.

Our usual sources had almost nothing to say on the subject of paths. Even the dictionary was useless; it didn't even point a direction. Our intuition told us that this was an enormously powerful symbol, although our first search for information was frustrated.

But we persevered and eventually found what we needed. When the gates of information finally opened, we discovered that our original intuition was right. The symbolism of the path is very rich and very important.

The essence of the matter is simply that a path facilitates the happening of whatever needs to happen. This is true on a physical level in the physical world for all sorts of creatures, including human beings, and it is even truer in the inner world of human beings. Paths in the physical world are simple. They need no explanation. But in the inner life of a human being, that simplicity gives way to the most extraordinary subtlety and complexity.

At this point, let's do a meditation.

Path Meditation

Breathe and relax.

Surround yourself with darkness and rest there for awhile.

The darkness gives way to the soft light of the moon or to the light of the sun.

You find yourself in a landscape of forest, meadow, or mountainside. There are no other people around or signs of human habitation anywhere. A little way ahead you see the beginning of a path. Move towards it now.

Take a moment to observe the path without setting foot on it.

Soon you will follow the path for awhile, paying careful attention to everything you see along the way and how the experience of traveling the path makes you feel.

This will happen on your next breath.

(2-3 minutes) Follow the path wherever it leads.

It is time to leave this path for the time being. In a moment, you will step off the path, back into the comforting darkness from which you began. This will happen on your next breath.

As you cloak yourself in the familiar darkness, breathe and relax. Slowly become aware of your physical body and your current surroundings, and when you are ready, open your eyes.

• • •

The first step we need to take in understanding the nature of a path is to define it, which we'll do even without the help of a dictionary. The definition of a thing is often found at the boundary between what it is and what it is not, and that's where we'll begin. We'll make our way from this general beginning through some powerful examples from a variety of places and cultures to the paths of tarot and the particular paths in specific cards.

Let's start with a useful question. How do you know a path when you see one? Here are some of the ways:

1. A path is a natural part of a natural landscape. It is not paved, and there's no sign of any organized effort to create it.

2. A path is distinct from its landscape—it is figure to the landscape's ground. You can see a path and know for sure that it exists. It is not ambiguous or unclear.

3. A path is made by the passage of many living feet, guided by the same intention.

4. A path is narrow, allowing for the passage of only a single individual at a time.

5. A path is unmarked, other than by the clarity of its contrast with the landscape through which it passes. It is unregulated, unpoliced, unattended. Passage over it is a matter of personal choice or personal destiny.

6. A path does not have to be traveled from end to end. It does not insist on completion. The reason for traveling it may be either a goal or an experience.

7. What can be said of a physical path can also be said of a symbolic one.

A path is not a road.

1. A road is an intentional creation, made by the organized effort of a few on behalf of many.

2. A road is regulated, organized, and maintained, again, by the few on behalf of the many.

3. The purpose of a road is to facilitate rapid and easy passage from beginning to end. It is not meant to facilitate experience, except as a possible by-product of traveling to a chosen destination.

4. A road invites rapid rather than languorous movement, and it frowns on departure from its way and its rules. A road is public and allows only what is proper in public.

5. A road encourages simultaneous and constant use by the many to justify the time, effort, and resources of the few who created and maintain it.

A path is not a way, although sometimes one becomes the other.

1. A way exists only as the report of one who has experienced it. It cannot be seen or experienced without such a report, and it cannot be traveled without a guide.

2. A way is the means of passage across shifting landscapes or abstract distances—like water, sand, and sky or the farthest reaches of mind, soul, and spirit.

3. No one would travel such a way if they were not intentionally tempted with the benefits of completing it. The benefits of completing a way are also known only to one who has accomplished it and are available only on the report of such a one.

4. Traveling a way needs faith, since both the way and its reasons are invisible to the uninitiated eye.

5. Because a way only exists for the potential traveler as a matter of faith, it is subject to possible abuse. Reports of a way can be claimed without basis, and guides for such a way may be frauds or fools. To trust a reported way leads to the danger of being gulled. But to be skeptical leads to the danger of losing the possibility of a great benefit.

A path, with its clear delineation against the background of a known landscape, may become a way in the end. But then it is a necessary and inevitable continuation of something you have come to trust, and so it may be trusted as well.

At this point, when a path loses itself in a way, the two together may become transmuted into a journey.

A journey is not a path, though it may include one.

1. A journey is long and may involve both paths and ways.

2. A journey is a commitment to a long-term goal and fails if the goal is not reached. But a path may be traveled at the convenience of the traveler and does not require completion.

3. While a journey allows for and even encourages experience, all experience is in the service of the goal. A path permits and encourages experience for its own sake. What is experienced along a path may become more important than the original reason for traveling it.

4. A journey is a line, and its end is far from its beginning. A path may be circular or meandering, and its end may be near or the same as its beginning.

Paths and roads, ways and journeys originate in the physical world, but from time immemorial, they have been internalized in humanity's deepest experience of itself. Of all the inner paths in the world, the ones that are well documented and well traveled, there are a few we want to share with you, because each in its own way gives useful insights into the paths in tarot.

All of these are spiritual paths in one way or another. Their common essence is that they all point to some version of escape from the dilemma of the suffering small self in the great world, and they all lead, at the very least, to magnificent self-improvement and refinement. We'll start in the East and work our way westward.

The Noble Eightfold Path of Buddhism

One of the most famous of all spiritual paths is actually a manifold of several aspects. The Buddhist Noble Eightfold Path cuts across the landscape of Buddha's Four Noble Truths—which are actually kind of depressing at first glance. We'll give you the list, and you can see for yourself:

1. Life means suffering.

2. The origin of suffering is attachment.

3. The cessation of suffering is attainable.

4. The path to the cessation of suffering is the Eightfold Path.

Needless to say, the landscape of the Four Noble Truths deserves a lengthy explanation, but we can only give you a glimpse of it here. The origin of suffering is said to be attachment to transient things, and all things in this world are said to be transient. This includes not only physical things but also ideas and all the objects of our perception. The essence of suffering is contained in two words: craving and clinging. With a little bit of thought, anyone can apply this idea to their own life. The themes of craving and clinging, in one way or another, appear in most tarot readings.

The Eightfold Path is Buddhism's answer to the dilemma of its Four Noble Truths. The eight parts of this path are as follows:

1. Right View

2. Right Intention

3. Right Speech

4. Right Action

5. Right Livelihood

6. Right Effort

7. Right Mindfulness

8. Right Concentration

The Noble Eightfold Path is a practical guide to personal freedom from attachments and delusions. Together with the Four Noble Truths it is the essence of Buddhism. Here is a brief explanation of the eight aspects of this path, which you can probably apply to your own life or the lives of your querents.

The first aspect is *Right View,* and it means to see and understand things as they really are and to realize the Four Noble Truths. It means to grasp the impermanence and imperfectness of the world of objects and concepts. The things you have won't last all that long, and maybe the things you want aren't all that great.

The second aspect is *Right Intention,* the commitment to ethical and mental self-improvement. Buddha names three types of right intention:

a. the intention to renounce desire,

b. the intention of good will,

c. the intention to do no harm.

The third path is *Right Speech,* which Buddha explains as follows:

a. to abstain from falsehood,

b. to abstain from slander,

c. to abstain from offensive and hurtful words,

d. to abstain from idle chatter.

The fourth aspect is called *Right Action*, which involves the body. Unwholesome physical actions are said to lead to unsound states of mind, while wholesome actions lead to sound states of mind. Right Action means:

a. to abstain from taking life (including your own)—don't kill anything;

b. to abstain from taking what is not freely given—don't steal, leach, or extort;

c. to abstain from self-indulgence—in food, drink, sex, drugs, etc.

The fifth aspect is *Right Livelihood*, which means that one should earn one's living in a righteous, legal, and peaceful way. The Buddha mentions four specific activities that harm other beings and that should be avoided:

a. dealing in weapons,

b. dealing in living beings such as slave trade and prostitution,

c. working in meat production and butchery,

d. selling intoxicants and poisons, such as alcohol and drugs.

The sixth aspect is *Right Effort*, which is an act of will without which nothing positive can be achieved. Right Effort is described as four acts of mental discipline:

a. prevent the acquisition of bad habits,

b. abandon the bad habits you already have,

c. acquire good habits,

d. maintain and perfect good habits and qualities you already have.

Right Mindfulness is the seventh aspect, and it's the one Wald is particularly drawn to. It is the ability to see things without distortion. What we think we know begins with an impression induced by a sense perception. We take this impression and instantly conceptualize and interpret it. The mind then joins concepts into constructs and weaves those constructs into elaborate interpretative schemes. All this happens much faster than conscious thought, and the result is that what we actually see is obscured by an impenetrable web of interpretation. Right Mindfulness is a clear perception that dissolves this interpretive net and allows us to see what's behind it. This process is crucial but very hard to learn.

The last aspect of the Eightfold Path is *Right Concentration,* which is simply one-pointedness of mind. With training, the mind learns to focus, to intensify, and finally to sustain concentration on a chosen act or object to achieve a clear and fruitful vision. Easy to say, very hard to do.

Obviously, this is only the most skeletal description of a set of practices that may take a dedicated Buddhist a lifetime to learn. Following the Eightfold Path creates tremendous mental and spiritual refinement even if it isn't traveled to the end. Taken all the way, it leads ultimately to Nirvana.

We spent quite a bit of time talking about this particular path because it gives in detail the essence of the same practical goal of what in the West is commonly called the Path of Ascent. It explicitly describes the world as a place of suffering we would all be well advised to escape, and it gives a way to make this happen through a step-by-step program of spiritual discipline and elevation.

The Great Path of Return

There is a parallel and contemporary tradition in the culture of India that is called the Great Path of Return, the path of yogis, saints, and sages. It is a path that takes the traveler deeper and deeper inward. It is the path that leads to the heart and finally to enlightenment at the center of the seeker's very own self.

Yogis specialize in refining the original physical condition through controlling and manipulating the current of life energy known as prana, or breath, and the energy known as kundalini, which rises from the lowest chakra at the base of the spine to the crown chakra at the top of the head. This is a physical path of ascent that seeks to enter the subtle dimension of divine light.

The Indian saints bypass energy manipulation, including controlling kundalini, and begin with concentration on the internal sound and light of the subtle dimension behind the brows. The path of the saints is unconcerned with improving bodily karma, since its goal is to move completely beyond the level of physical existence. Experience on this path begins with the sublime and goes deeper from there.

Finally, there's the causal path, the path of the sages. They go straight to the dimension of manifest consciousness without either subtle or physical experiences. This path is an intense enquiry directly into the nature of consciousness itself, without manipulating energies of any kind in either the mind or body. The sages' focus is on consciousness before any manifestation, in its first modification as the separate self-sense, the ego—"I." This is a path of pure transcendent meditation and contemplation—the highest, most abstract, most demanding, and most inward of the Indian paths of return, and its experiences are said to be beyond description.

What all of these paths have in common that they look for the essence concealed in appearances. The goal of all these paths is to arrive at the heart, the intuitive center of consciousness. This is called realization.

Every form and appearance, every feeling and perception, every thought, every vision, everything experienced above, beyond, or within, is said to appear first in the heart and then as the play of manifestation.

This direct intuition of the heart dissolves all the limitations of the sense of self, puts an end to all the suffering induced by limitation, and achieves a state of perfect enjoyment and serenity unaffected by any manifestation whatsoever. The achievement of such a state would clearly do away with any need for a tarot reading, but until then, tarot is a path that can actually help a person move in this direction.

The Path of Ascent

In the Middle East and the Mediterranean, the path from suffering in the world to elevated states of serene consciousness is called the Path of Ascent. With variations, it runs through Hermeticism, which is a Hellenized version of the Egyptian mysteries, as well as through early esoteric Christianity, Gnosticism, and Judaism. In its own way, each of these systems used the Path of Ascent for the same reason as their Indian counterpart: to escape inward to the center of being from the periphery. Their goal was to move through and past the obvious misery of worldly existence—what Christianity calls the vale of tears, what alchemy calls the gross primal material, what Gnostics saw as a kind of evil joke of the divine demiurge, and what certain aspects of Greek philosophy saw as the very bottom rung of the ladder of consciousness.

Rosicrucianism, Ceremonial Magick, Qabalah (both Jewish and Hermetic), Freemasonry, and later groups like the Golden Dawn all built on this earlier foundation. In all of these Western forms, a well-beaten path of practices like prayer, celibacy, and the induced visions of guided meditation could be followed by any seeker who wanted to move toward elevation and perfection. All the things we said earlier about paths as distinct from roads, ways, and journeys can be applied here.

But they all tended to give it a Western spin, changing the direction of the path from inward to upward, from an immanent deity to a transcendent one. The difference between immanent and transcendent is important philosophically, but they are the same path at their root.

The paths of tarot are no exception to these principles, although beyond a certain point, even the clearest path can give out. Familiar ground may turn into a trackless expanse, at which point a path becomes a way. Here, books and records and esoteric orders and communities can be of no further assistance to the traveler. Until this point is reached, if ever, tarot as a whole is a path as worthy as any ever traveled.

Of all the versions of the Western path of ascent, Hermetic Qabalah, embedded deepest in tarot lore, remains clear and can be followed to the greatest distance in the form of the paths of the Tree of Life. Those who have gone that way before say it is highly unlikely that the paths of the Tree will exhaust themselves before the traveler reaches the end of his or her energy.

This is the root of the intention and value of what, in tarot, is known as pathworking. Although this term also has a place in modern Neo-Pagan and shamanic practice, it is purely Qabalistic in the universe of tarot. Even pathworking is only one part of the path of tarot and not the one you can see in the cards.

Whatever is cultural form, the spiritual impulse that sets a person on a path exists in everyone, although it is stronger in some than in others. When a pictured path in a card catches your attention in a reading, it suggests the inner need to act on that impulse in some way.

This can take the form of a deep desire for inner refinement and improvement. There could be a desire for a return to an early and familiar spirituality or for the beginning of a new and attractive path, spiritual or otherwise. It suggests the desire to move inward and upward or perhaps the urge to experiment with a new and very significant change in lifestyle beyond anything that has been experienced up to now.

This is true in general, no matter which card with a path in it you're looking at, although each specific path has its own variation on the theme.

8 of Pentacles

Let's look first at the path in the 8 of Pentacles, between the foreground figure and the background city. This is path of the Freemason, although it doesn't necessarily involve Freemasonry at all. You must travel whatever path you have chosen step by step in an orderly and prescribed fashion, until you experience its mysteries in full and become what you are destined to become. The path is long, well trodden, and deeply satisfying to those inclined to travel it. It suggests discipline, effort, learning, and, ultimately, faith in what lies beyond it. And it guarantees the traveler, at the very least, a level of knowledge, understanding, and character far beyond the norm.

Ace of Pentacles

Next, we'll look at the path in the Ace of Pentacles, which takes the traveller from his or her own involvement deep in the ordinary world back toward the heights from which it came. What is important about this path is that what it leads to can only be guessed at, but it promises fabulous experiences along the way and a view of ultimate mysteries at the end. According to tarot, this is a path of awakening that everyone will feel drawn to follow sooner or later.

The Moon

Then we come to The Moon in the Major Arcana, which shows the path as an offer we can't refuse—the slow, perilous, necessary path of personal evolution. In the foreground are the difficulties we know and can predict. Further out is the vague and fearsome unknown, extending almost forever to the edges of consciousness. We don't choose this path; it chooses us, and we intuitively suspect we'll have to travel it to the end. It runs from the depths to the heights and promises us a reward equal to the difficulty of the journey.

Temperance

Finally, we reach the card of Temperance, where, after a tremendous amount of testing and strengthening, we are shown a path straight to glory, which we have earned the right to travel. This path seems to end just before it reaches the radiance that all inner paths seek. Beyond this ending there are no paths, no ways, no roads, no journeys. Beyond this point, nothing is left of the ordinary. The traveler, and his or her path, pass beyond description. This is as far as tarot can take you.

• • •

On all four of these pictured paths, travelers may well experience in their daily lives some aspects of the crown, the pillars, and the rose and the lily that we talked about in chapter one. The aspects of the crown, pillars, and rose and lily may also suggest issues and practices that arise on the paths of other traditions we have mentioned in this lesson, such as right livelihood, right effort, study and learning, prayer, and the enjoyment of traveling rather than focus on a goal. It is the purpose of the paths of tarot to bring us to these experiences.

When your attention is caught by a path in a reading, be aware of it as a beckoning, a seduction, a chance your querents can take, which may lead to experiences beyond anything they may have known before. Such experiences may or may not be spiritual, but they will be highly unusual and deeply satisfying. All that's needed is willingness, and the courage and resources will be supplied.

I want to bring this class to an end with my favorite quote about paths, which comes from Carlos Castaneda. His teacher tells him:

> Anything is one of a million paths. Therefore, a warrior must always keep in mind that a path is only a path; if he feels that he should not follow it, he must not stay with it under any conditions. His decision to keep on that path or to leave it must be free of fear or ambition. He must look at every path closely and deliberately. There is a question that a warrior has to ask, mandatorily: "Does this path have a heart?"
>
> All paths are the same, they lead nowhere. However a path without a heart is never enjoyable. On the other hand, a path with heart is easy—it does not make a warrior work at liking it; it makes for a joyful journey; as long as a man follows it, he is one with it.

MOUNTAINS

Welcome to our class on the image of the mountain in tarot. Mountains appear in at least twenty-five cards, of which we will discuss seven in class—the 10 of Swords, Judgement, The Moon, The Tower, Temperance, The Hermit, and The Lovers.

We're going to give you the end of the class first, like dessert before the vegetables, because we want this impression to be the first and most lasting.

The single most important thing to know about mountains is that they reach beyond the ordinary, and their presence lifts our consciousness above the ordinary even when they are far away. Up close, they don't just reach beyond the ordinary, they annihilate it, and they annihilate the ordinary in us as well.

But smallness is not just vaporized. It's replaced. At the top of a high mountain, a human being is released into the perspective of the roof of the world. The mountain's height becomes the person's height. All of the mountain's immensity enters the senses and transforms the consciousness of the beholder.

Beauty, strangeness, barrenness, utter extremes, and a spontaneous sense of the sacred; wind, ice, rock; cold and thinness and clarity of air; immense distances, spectacular colors, sudden engulfing storms; utter disinterest in the needs, or even in the existence, of life—all these are the hallmarks of a mountain peak's impact on human awareness.

In an environment as extreme, as magnificent, as deadly as this, a human being can survive for only a short while and even then only with the help of extraordinary skills, endurance, and strength. Simply to reach such an environment can be the ultimate test of personal strengths and weaknesses. Just to draw its experience into lungs, eyes, and heart is enough of a reason to undergo the effort and to take the risk to achieve it.

This is the essence of the mountain's meaning in tarot, although there are other less important issues connected with mountains in general and tarot mountains in particular. We need to know and understand these too, if we are to make the best intuitive use of mountains as a symbol.

In tarot, as in the world, mountains come singly, in pairs, and in ranges. But however they appear, if they're in your neighborhood, you have to deal with them. The most obvious characteristic of mountains is that, more than anything else, they totally dominate your vision. You can't miss them.

Mountains serve seven main functions for human beings. They are:

1. landmarks
2. boundaries
3. barriers
4. challenges
5. fortresses
6. retreats
7. habitable landscapes

Mountains may be observed, approached, climbed, passed over or through, dwelt on or dwelt within.

They are home to divinities of all sorts and cultures—mythical beings like trolls, ogres, gnomes, and dragons; seekers of wisdom and solitude, like recluses, monks, sages, and prophets; and a whole variety of outlaws, revolutionaries, robber barons, and adventurers, both secular and spiritual. And, of course, there are just plain folk who like to live there.

Tall mountains induce awe, worship, spontaneous ecstasy, and a sense of simultaneous elevation and separation. They annihilate self-importance and the small concerns of everyday life. There is no sense that a human being, or, for that matter, any living thing, belongs here. High peaks are barren, lifeless, often brilliant with snow and ice.

Mountains test your strengths, reveal your weaknesses, protect and hide you, elevate, separate, and purify you. They give you a locale for your sacred stories and fairy tales and a symbol for your purest endeavors, highest goals, and greatest efforts.

If this were a six-week course of three-hour days and five-day weeks, and we could spend all that time together just on this one image of the mountain, at the end of that time I believe we would all be changed forever. We would need a six-week course to fully discuss all the things we have mentioned about mountains so far.

Earlier, we said that mountains in tarot come individually and in ranges and pairs. As usual with tarot imagery, they mean different things in different cards. Since there are so many of them, we'll look at just a few of the more interesting ones.

There are, as we mentioned before, at least twenty-five cards that have mountains in them in some form and possibly more. We say possibly because sometimes there is only the barest visual hint, and it's hard to tell if you're seeing a mountain or not. The seven we'll briefly mention are the most prominent or most representative of a mountain issue. Six of these are Majors and one is a Minor.

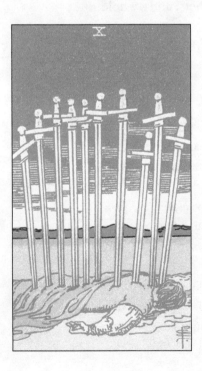

10 of Swords

Let's begin with the mountains in the 10 of Swords. Their message is simple. They are as far as the eye can see. They are the edge of what you can know. What's beyond them is anybody's guess and will always be a mystery. This use of a mountain range as the symbol of a boundary or limit is a theme repeated in several other cards.

Judgement

Now let's look at Judgement. The mountains here are solid ice, as harsh an environment as you can get. But the symbolism is pure Qabalah. Remember that every tarot trump is a path on the Tree of Life, and this is one of the first paths that leads up and out of the ordinary world. Its destination is a place of ice-cold intelligence where the laws of nature are made. It's a place of mind but not heart, a very lofty and rigorous landscape, not intended to provide the least bit of comfort or safety.

But the path of Judgement is a path of fire that keeps the traveler warm enough to live even in such a place and pass beyond it into the unknown. The mountains of Judgement are the goal of the experience of awakening, and you go there because they hold crucial knowledge you need to learn.

The Moon

Next are the mountains of The Moon. They are far away at the end of a long and scary path you have to travel, but they are what make the trip worthwhile. Those mountains are the symbol of the treasure and blessing of growing up, of full maturity. At the top of those mountains stands the peak of The Hermit, intimately joined to the path of The Moon in a birth card pairing, promising you the achievement of your highest goals. The mountains of The Moon are a symbol of ultimate reward for patience, effort, determination, and courage.

65

The Tower

The mountains in Judgement were tough and so is the forbidding mountain peak of The Tower. Here, the mountain is literally a peak experience. This is the absolute highest point you can reach as a natural physical and psychological human being. It is the symbol of the roof of the natural world. And, of course, on the roof is the lightning rod of an ambition to reach beyond the limits of nature. But beyond this point, you run the almost certain risk of being struck down by the deadly storms of unknown forces. You can't stop here, but you can't go on as you are. This mountain demands that something major in you has to change.

Temperance

Moving upward on the path of ascent, assuming you got past the lightning bolts at the roof of the natural world, you enter the world of spirit on the path of Temperance. Before you even get settled in your newly elevated spiritual condition, you see in the far distance of Temperance the twin peaks of a condition beyond even the spiritual. These are the two transcendent pillars of Wisdom and Understanding leading straight to the experience of Glory, which crowns the Tree of Life.

Here, the mountains are a statement that you have already come farther than you ever dreamed, that this is not a time to rest but to keep moving, that you have the strength to finish what you began a long time ago.

The Hermit

In The Hermit, another peak has been reached, and the spirit now stands beneath the open sky with nothing beyond but the endless vastness of transcendent space. This is the final accomplishment of the spirit: to have arrived where nothing is visible beyond what you have achieved. This mountain peak is the place where spirit and transcendence touch, far above even the imagination of the natural world where you began your journey in the landscape of The Moon. You have gone as far as effort can carry you. Beyond this point, you cannot go without the help of a higher power.

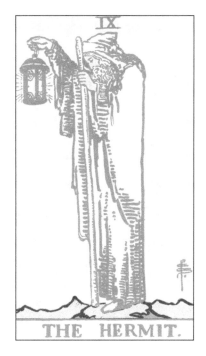

The Lovers

We'll end the journey of this particular lesson with the single mountain in the landscape of The Lovers. It rises to meet a welcoming archangel, who brings the battle of the sexes, all the endless oppositions of the masculine and feminine pillars, to a resolution in an orgasm of union. It is the final act of healing, and the mountain is the experience of coming home at last.

• • •

The mountains we have looked at in this class are only a few of the mountain experiences in the deck, but they give you an idea of the scope and importance of the image of the mountain in tarot.

Each example describes an experience of climbing, each to a higher place than the one before it. Together, they beg the question "What do I do with this information in a reading?" But that question lives on the surface of a deeper issue, which needs to be addressed before the question itself can be answered. And that brings us to the closing of this class.

We want to end by reminding you of where we began, with the awareness of the mountain as a symbol of transcendent personal experience, of the human condition in an extraordinary rather than an ordinary state.

Tarot is normally used as a tool for dealing with the ordinary events of ordinary life, all-important to people in an ordinary state. This covers most people and most happenings most of the time. But one of the problems that tarot faces is that many who study and use tarot concern themselves with nothing else. Their interest and faith is in the small and practical. That is how they see themselves, others, and the world. They know theoretically that there's more to the world than the ordinary human condition, but that is such a remote consideration for them that they are not inclined to bother with it.

Mountains are a symbol of what is extraordinary, what is beyond the normal in all things, and they appear in more cards than perhaps any other image in tarot. This is a reminder that the vast, the sacred, the awesome, the mighty, the unknown, and the transcendent are a part of the natural human condition as often as not.

It's a good idea to be aware that any reading may ascend to the extraordinary at any time without notice. It is also good to know that, as a reader (if you know how), you have the option of offering your querent the gift of the extraordinary for the taking. In our opinion, this is the final lesson of the mountain in tarot. We'll get a chance to discuss some of the down-to-earth lessons of the mountain in the integration class at the end of this series.

CROSSES

Welcome to our class on crosses in tarot. Crosses appear in the following cards: The High Priestess, The Empress, The Emperor, The Hierophant, The Hanged Man, Death, Judgement, the Ace of Cups, the 6 of Cups, and the 3 of Pentacles.

As you know, our last two classes were on the symbols of the path and the mountain, and those two have a couple of things in common. First, they are both natural forms found in natural landscapes. Mountains are made out of the movements of the earth's crust, and paths are made by the movement of living feet over the earth's surface.

They are also alike because their naturalness is a complete contrast with the image of the cross, which springs straight out of the human mind. If there is one symbol of distilled human consciousness, the cross is it.

Why, it has been asked from ancient times, did the chicken cross the road? When Caesar crossed the Rubicon, Rome changed forever. Romeo and Juliet were star-crossed lovers, the model of romantic love for the whole world. The Voodoo god Elegua and Greek goddess Hecate are deities in charge of crossroads, where all-important decisions are made. The most hidden personal truths and motives are uncovered by cross-examination. Perfect strangers become important to each other when their paths cross. To cross the ocean is to go as far as one can physically go in this world. When two people cross swords, a battle is joined. A double-cross is the essence of treachery.

When a cross is tilted, it becomes an X. An X in a box signifies that a choice has been made. An X on a signature line is a universal sign of human identity, and X marks the spot on every map of buried treasure.

In language, the cross is a super-rich symbol of human relationships. But a graphic cross carries us into the abstract universe of mathematics, logic, and philosophy. And that's before we even get to spirituality. We'll touch on some of that here, though it will have to be just a touch because we know very close to nothing about the subjects mentioned above. Even so, there are some interesting ideas we can look at that can be useful in tarot.

The Cross as a Graphic

The whole idea of a cross is the absolute contrast of opposites. Graphically, a cross is drawn as the intersection of two lines moving in directions as totally different from each other as we can see or conceive. And this is the first and most important thing to remember about a cross in the context of tarot. It's just a picture of the meeting of two things that couldn't be more opposite. This is the image of opposites as a creative interaction, rather than as sterile parallels that never meet or as useless head-on collisions.

The two directions of a cross are so radically different from each other that each one is experienced as a whole separate dimension. They literally make the first two dimensions of the space we all live in. The second important thing to remember about a cross is that it shows us a universe we could never get to from one perspective alone. It's a universe that lets us create on a whole new level, and it's often built out of the opposing energies of an irreconcilable argument.

The third thing that a cross gives us is something else that one perspective alone doesn't contain. Where the two directions intersect is a point, a center, which has no dimension at all. But it serves a vital function. It is an infinite and eternal fountain, the source of the four arms of the cross, each of which arises and takes its energy from the center. To begin with, a cross is made of a simple pair of opposites. When the opposites cross, they make a pair of pairs, the double duality that is one of the deepest secrets of tarot. From the amazing fountainhead of its center, a cross generates all the complications of the world.

Just for fun, let's bring up something that you may never have thought of. When a cross spins on its center, perpendicular (at right angles) to its two original directions, it creates the third dimension of the world we all experience as physical space. This is a cross with three arms that extends in three totally different directions at once. The result is a world infinitely enriched by another absolute difference.

Now imagine adding a fourth direction to the cross, perpendicular to the first three. This would be the addition of another absolute difference, another dimension. The theory has it that, for us, three dimensions are the most we can experience as a stable state, which we call space, and the fourth dimension is experienced as change, as the flow of time. The theory goes on to suggest that a being that lives in any stable perception experiences what is totally different from and just beyond that perception as change. Each part of our experience, both moving and still, is made of the intersection of directions, or possibilities, as different from each other as the universe is capable of making them.

The lesson here is that a cross is the symbol of all that changes and all that stays the same. It is the relationship between the stable state of things as they are, represented by the horizontal line, and the dynamic state of things as they might become, represented by the vertical. It is the symbol of the creative potential of absolute difference.

Now let's begin to draw these interesting abstractions down to the level of tarot.

The Cross in Tarot

Sometimes, the cross functions more as four arms extending from a center than as two lines intersecting. In such a cross, all the arms have equal significance and so they are shown as having equal length. This is called an equal-armed cross. It suggests stability, the sum total of all there is, and it's a universal symbol of serenity.

Sometimes a cross is made of the simple intersection of a vertical and horizontal line, giving more extension to the vertical line than to the horizontal and more length to one end of the vertical than to the other. It turns verticality from an equal partner in a stable universe into a force of dynamic change. This is what is called a Latin cross, the symbol of a particular spirituality, and it suggests dissatisfaction with things as they are and the need to improve them.

There are examples of both kinds of cross in tarot.

The High Priestess

Perhaps the most famous cross in tarot is the equal-armed cross of The High Priestess. It combines Hermetic with Qabalistic tradition; it is rich in significance but simple to describe. It is the central secret of the guardian of secrets, and its place is over the priestess's heart.

Its four arms contain all the secrets of the number four. It refers to all the fours of the natural world, like directions, seasons, moon phases, etc., and also to more hidden symbolism, like the Tetragrammaton and its four Hebrew letters. The whole world, and all of tarot, is said to spring from these and other sets of four.

There is more than one lesson in the cross of The High Priestess, but the most important is that each of the four arms is equal. North is as good as south, winter is as good as spring, old age serves as great a purpose as childhood. Pain and pleasure, fullness and emptiness, even life and death, are equal. A hard lesson to learn, but it's the one that brings serenity and balance into your life.

The Hierophant

The Hierophant has one of the more intriguing crosses in the deck. It is the papal triple cross, symbol of the three realms of spirit over which the Catholic Church presides. The first realm, which is symbolized by the lowest bar of the cross, is called the Church Militant. It converts, organizes, and leads the masses. It moves people into the fold and keeps them moving in the right direction.

The second bar is for the Church Penitent, the world of angels and of souls waiting for birth or judgment. Here, the church teaches and forms the mind and spirit to make it worthy of its destiny.

The third bar is for the Church Triumphant, realm of the archangels, heaven, and the reward of the virtuous.

The same triple cross contains the hierarchy of the three Masonic degrees. The Entered Apprentice learns to live in harmony with his physical and social environment. The Fellowcraft refines his mind and spirit. The Master Mason strives to live in an elevated state of completion and serenity.

This vertical cross contrasts with the equal-armed cross of The High Priestess. The simple lesson of this cross is patience and effort. The highest condition or best state available to you is achieved step by step, in an orderly way, with persistent effort over time.

6 of Cups

Another unusual cross appears in a heraldic field on the stone pedestal in the 6 of Cups. First, it is the tilted cross of St. Andrew, a martyr's cross. Second, it said to be the coat of arms of Johann Valentine Andreae, author of one of three primary Rosicrucian texts, *The Chemical Wedding of Christian Rosenkreutz*, which is a description of the alchemical sacrifice of the legendary founder of the Rosicrucian Order. And third, it is a reference to the esoteric title of the 6 of Cups, the Lord of Pleasure. It is the X that marks the spot that gives the greatest pleasure in any situation.

In this reference, ecstasy is connected with martyrdom and sacrifice. The Qabalistic reference here is to the 6 of Cups as Beauty in the world of Creation, sometimes called the Christ center at the heart of the Tree of Life. The two messages for the tarot reader in this cross are first that the greatest pleasure and the greatest reward is in giving and second that the best thing to give is pleasure—spiritual, emotional, mental, or physical.

• • •

Finally, we'll talk about two related crosses that don't really look like crosses at all. But one is important for understanding tarot, and the other is important for understanding life itself.

The Hanged Man

THE HANGED MAN.

The Tau cross of The Hanged Man is the first of these. Tau is the Greek name for the letter T, and its importance comes from two factors. (It's odd, isn't it, how the number two keeps coming up when we talk about crosses?) First, in early Christianity, when the Latin cross was not yet the symbol of the Roman Church and the Greek cross was not yet the symbol of the Eastern Church, the true cross was said to be the Tau cross. And this is also for two reasons.

First, this is the way crosses were actually constructed by the Romans for the purpose of execution, and it was what Jesus was crucified on. The long part, called the stipes, was set permanently in the ground. In difficult times and places in the Roman Empire, there were whole forests of these implanted verticals ready for use as needed. The crosspiece was called the patibulum. It weighed about 100 pounds, and the condemned person had to carry it himself to the place of execution—hence his name, the patibulatus.

After the patibulatus carried the crosspiece of his cross out to the field of execution, he'd be attached to it with ropes or with nails. Then he'd be hauled up so that the patibulum could be fastened to the stipes. We usually think of the two pieces being nicely joined with each other to form the Latin cross shape. But the Roman army carpenters, who had hundreds and thousands of crosses to make, didn't bother with that kind of fancy carpentry. They just affixed a peg in the top of the stipes and bored a hole through the center of the patibulum that fit over the peg. That made it easy to assemble the cross in a single motion. The weight of the crossbeam and the crucified man held the cross together, resulting in a shape like the Greek letter Tau.

The second reason the true cross was said to be Tau shaped is that the Roman empress Helena is said to have found the true original cross, which was shaped like a Tau, buried under a temple of Aphrodite in Jerusalem. She supposedly had it shipped back to Rome, and splinters of this "true cross" were distributed as sacred relics to churches all over the empire. Skeptics point out that the combined amount of wood in those splinters would have made a cross big enough to sink the ship that carried it.

The second factor that gives the Tau cross its importance is that the Hebrew letter for T, which is Tav, is the last letter of the Hebrew alphabet. It isn't T-shaped in Hebrew, but it is in Greek, and the Greek translation of the Old Testament is the foundation of formal Christianity, both east and west.

Jesus was, therefore, crucified on what was seen as the shape of the final expression of Judaism, and he is said to have thereby reversed the fall of man and redeemed the world with his sacrifice. The Tau cross has come in this way to be seen as the symbol of redemption through the act of reversal. This whole idea is graphically suggested in The Hanged Man of tarot.

The simple lesson here is that an impossible or unacceptable situation can be saved by reversing it, by seeing it from a whole new perspective. This corresponds with the idea that the second direction of a cross adds a new dimension to any situation and a new solution to any problem.

The Emperor

From the intensity of the Tau cross of The Hanged Man we come to a very different sensibility in the Ankh of The Emperor.

An Ankh is a Tau cross with a circle or loop above it. This is a very old and much venerated Egyptian symbol and actually comes long before the cross. It is a hieroglyphic picture of the masculine vertical line rising through the feminine horizon and being transformed into the immortal rising sun. The Ankh has always been an amulet of pharaohs and kings that brings life, health, happiness, and fortune to those who possess it. The lesson of the Ankh is that simple.

• • •

The cross in all these cards has many levels of interpretation beyond the ones we've given, but sadly, we don't have room here to get past the surface. And of course there are all the other cards with crosses on them that we mentioned earlier, which we didn't even get to talk about at all.

For now, it is enough to know that every cross in tarot opens a door not just to issues but to whole dimensions. All the inner languages and landscapes that together make tarot what it is are on the other side of just such doors, waiting for you to find them, open them, and walk through them.

That sounds like both a simple and a difficult task and, for some, an attractive one.

To accomplish it, you just need to follow a path and climb a mountain.

INTEGRATION:
PATHS, MOUNTAINS, AND CROSSES

"Hello and welcome." Those first few words are, to us, the most pleasant and most important words to say and hear in any lesson: "Hello and welcome."

This class is an integration of all that we have discussed together in the three lessons of this chapter. We stood together in a waterfall of information and ideas, but our experience has been that in a learning situation like this, we get wet but absorb little. An integration class is intended to let us soak in what we've heard, so that we can give it to others when they need to hear it in a reading and so that we have it for ourselves when we need it.

In past lessons, we've talked about the wedding of above and below, the commitment to the best in ourselves; about initiation, the difference between outside and inside, and how transforming it is to make the passage from one to the other through the process of learning; and about discovering the beauty and pleasure to be found on the path that lies between the two sides of an argument. All these things are learned from the images of the crowns, the pillars, and the rose and the lily.

Now we come to the path, the mountain, and the cross—all they have taught us and all we have to learn from them.

In the first integration class we did together, we used the method of recapitulating the information from earlier classes at length. Your task was to read, make notes and comments, and remember.

This time, we'll do it a little differently. It would give us the greatest pleasure and do you the most good to take a more active role in absorbing the lessons of the past three lessons. So we'll remind you briefly of the most important general issues of the images we've studied, but then it will be time for you to go inside to find a connection between the images and your own thoughts and experiences.

Here's a little secret about learning. It's a secret you may have heard before, but it bears repeating. To truly learn something and deeply possess it, you need to contemplate what you want to remember and understand.

So, after a little discussion, each of us is going to do a little contemplation, and we'll see where that takes us. We think you'll be pleased with what happens.

To begin with, you need to have in front of you the fourteen cards we've looked at in the last three lessons. They are:

The High Priestess
The Emperor
The Hierophant
The Lovers
The Hermit
The Hanged Man
Temperance
The Tower
The Moon
Judgement
Ace of Pentacles
8 of Pentacles
6 of Cups
10 of Swords

The cards with paths are The Moon, Temperance, and the Ace and 8 of Pentacles.

Mountains appear in The Lovers, The Hermit, Temperance, The Tower, The Moon, Judgement, and the 10 of Swords.

Crosses are in The High Priestess, The Emperor, The Hierophant, The Hanged Man, and the 6 of Cups.

All together, they make a single powerful lesson.

Each of us learns the lessons of the same cards in a different way. Another secret worth telling is that the world, and the things in it, are as you see them. The things we're about to say are the lessons for us in the cards we mentioned. Whether they are the same for you remains for you to discover.

Paths

The path is a path for each of us alone, no matter how many have traveled it before us or will travel it after us. It is there for us to experience what it has to teach us, and any path we choose to explore may be good for a short time or a long one, depending on whether or not it is a path that has heart for us. And that, of course, is for each of us to decide alone. A path always offers, never demands, although to follow a path with heart may ask of us all that we have to give.

Mountains

Mountains bear the message of the extravagant, the outsized, the superlative. Although individual mountains differ from each other as much as individual people, they all offer a goal, a challenge, a horizon, and a boundary. They all show us what we would look like, what life would be like, if we allowed ourselves to live the extraordinary instead of the ordinary. Mountains, unlike paths, are very demanding by their nature, and what they demand of us is that we live at the top of our game.

Crosses

Crosses bring to us all the layers of suggestion that can be found in a good dictionary or thesaurus, and they all apply beautifully to the affairs of everyday life. The adventure of crossing a threshold, the challenge of crossing a line drawn in the sand, the consequences of choosing a direction at a crossroads, the delight in each other of star-crossed lovers, the weight of a cross one has to bear, the anticipation of treasure when X (another kind of cross) marks the spot on a map, the sense of decision when an X in a box marks an important choice. And, of course, the crosses of pantheism and the religions of transcendence are all-important symbols of personal spirituality.

To all of these standard cultural references, add the cross's function of revealing dimensions, offering fresh perspectives, and opening up whole new possibilities for creativity, personal refinement, and spiritual elevation, and the cross becomes an amazing intuitive tool in a reading.

• • •

These few reminders about the themes of the images should be enough to help you remember the specific variations in the different cards where they appear. And they will also serve as a springboard for the contemplation exercise we are about to do.

Symbol Contemplation

First, close your eyes, breathe, and relax.

Surround yourself with darkness and let your mind rest.

Empty your mind of thoughts in a casual and comfortable way, and float peacefully for a few moments.

When you are ready, take a deep breath, open your eyes, but remain in a meditative state.

Now look at the fourteen cards face up in front of you. Let your eye intuitively choose the seven cards that are most pleasing or make the greatest impact on you at this moment. Separate them and put the others aside, face down.

Now look again at the seven cards you have chosen, and of these, choose the four that are the most important to you at this moment. Put the rest aside, face down.

From the four remaining cards, pick one to contemplate and put the rest aside face down, but keep them where you can find them easily.

Now look at the one card you have chosen from all the rest and focus on an image in that card that we have studied—a path, a mountain, or a cross.

Let that image enter you consciousness. Close your eyes, bring the image to mind, and ask yourself, "What is the meaning and the importance to me of this path, mountain, or cross?"

When you have asked yourself this question, listen for any answer that comes to you. The answer may come as a message you hear, see, or experience. Take a minute to do this, and remember any answer you receive.

The time has come to return and record your contemplation. Take a deep breath and, when you're ready, open your eyes. Now take a moment to write down what you have seen, heard, or experienced in your contemplation.

We've heard it said, and our experience confirms it, that nothing bears fruit without contemplation. Make a note of the other three cards you chose from among all the rest and, in your own time, contemplate the appropriate image in each one. We promise you that the results will be rewarding.

SYMBOL SPREAD:
CROSSROADS, PATH, AND MOUNTAIN

This spread makes use of the concepts discussed in the classes on the crosses, paths, and mountains, and it is ideally suited for readings involving overcoming an obstacle or achieving a goal. The layout is made up of three separate parts—the Crossroads, consisting of four cards; the Path, consisting of four cards; and the Mountain, consisting of three cards.

The Crossroads

To begin, shuffle your deck and divide it into four piles. Next, keeping the cards face down, arrange the piles into the shape of an equal-armed cross with an open space in the center like this:

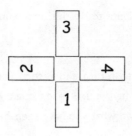

Turn over the top card of each pile and orient it so that the bottom of the card is at the center of the cross.

Contemplate these four cards and choose the one whose energy best reflects the direction you wish to go at this time. It may be that this direction shows the most promise in helping you achieve a goal, or it may signify the lure of something important or mysterious.

Indicate the card/direction you have chosen by turning the three other cards face down again.

Leaving the card you have chosen face up in the Crossroads, take the cards out from under it and hold them. You will draw the rest of the cards from this portion of the deck.

The Path

Take four cards from the top of the little stack of cards you are holding and arrange them in a Path pattern to the right of the Crossroads. You can play with the shape of your path, but we suggest something like this:

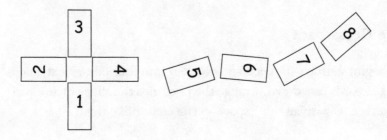

The nature of this path can be external or internal. The cards may suggest actions to perform and things to consider or observe along the way. They might represent events you'll encounter and the best way to respond to them internally as you continue on your journey. The cards that make up the Path benefit from contemplation. Even when their message seems clear at first glance, their deeper meaning will often be revealed over time.

The Mountain

The Mountain is made of the next three cards in the stack. Place them at the end of the Path, two on the bottom and one on top, like this:

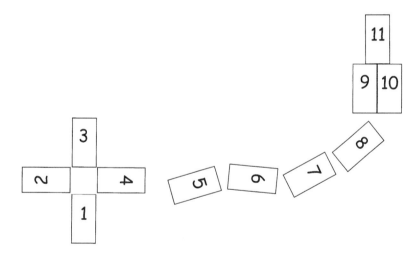

The three cards describe the way to climb the Mountain of the goal you are reaching for or the obstacle you are striving to overcome. These cards will also give you hints as to the best approach to take.

Additional Considerations

If your goal is not realistic or attainable at this time, the cards that compose the Crossroads will let you know. If none of the four cards present a clear or acceptable choice of direction, it would probably be best to wait awhile and try the reading again at another time.

If more than one card looks good to you, chances are you'll find success more than one way. However, take the time to contemplate the cards and choose the direction that has the strongest pull.

3

MOONS, STARS, POOLS

MOONS

We should begin by telling you that we have a love affair with the moon. So this class will be more of a contemplation than a lesson, more personal and less formal than usual.

From the ancient moment when consciousness first took human form, the moon, the sun, and the earth were felt inwardly as the family from which we sprang. They were the first and most universal of all symbols, and they may well have been the source of the human propensity to create symbols. In most places and times in human history they have been mother, father, and child, outwardly in nature and inwardly as our sense of ourselves.

With very few exceptions, human beings have always seen the moon as feminine. Wherever and whenever nature is deified, the moon is the goddess. She is the woman in us all.

She rules the night and all that is dark within us. She rules the sea and all that is tidal within us. She rules time and all that changes within us. She rules the circle and all that repeats itself within us.

Moon Contemplation

For a long moment, conjure the moon as she appears to you.

Close your eyes, breathe, and relax. Surround yourself with darkness, and let all your thoughts and feelings dissolve into shadows. Rest in this darkness and float there for awhile.

The time has come for the moon to rise in the night sky of your awareness. See her within you. Feel her light. Let it illumine the darkness inside you. For the next couple of minutes, look at, feel, know, and explore your inner moonlit landscape.

The time has come to return.

Let the moon move slowly downward in your inner night. Let darkness once again surround you, and rest there for a moment.

Become aware of your surroundings. Flex your fingers and toes. Take two deep breaths, and when you're ready, open your eyes.

Take a minute or two to write down your experience, and what it means to you.

• • •

All the things you have felt and seen and thought are personal. They are a quick first look at the moon as she lives inside of you. We began our class with this personal experience because one of the essential qualities of the moon is that she is personal. She is intimate and close, both in nature and as a symbol.

But because she is and has always been an intimate experience of every human being, she has been written and thought about, described and objectified, as much as any object or experience in the totality of human awareness.

The moon is the subject of poetry and science, religion and magic, love and madness. Each of these categories has its own characteristic vocabulary. Each is valid in its own way and has its own consequences for our lives.

The moon is the nearest of heavenly bodies. It has therefore been the target of humanity's first successful attempt to leave the earth in a physical manner, using all the power of science and technology and all the courage of adventure and exploration. Reaching the physical moon has given us, for the first time in history, another place to stand. It could well be a quantum leap in our evolution as a species.

Remember this when your eye is drawn to a moon in a card when you're doing a reading.

In astrology, the moon is also the nearest of heavenly bodies, the most intimate of personal planets, the first and most exhaustively observed of the lights in the sky and in ourselves.

In Qabalah, the moon is associated with the number nine in a series of ten. It is spiritually, as it is physically, the first step upward in the journey of human evolution, what in tarot is called the journey of return.

For Freemasonry and alchemy, the moon is a full and essential partner in the division of life into its necessary polarities and also in the process of healing and spiritual and magical union, which is understood to be the goal of the human spirit.

These are also things to remember about the moon in a reading.

The moon in poetry and drama, myth and psychology, is the face of the divine feminine—of romance, mystery, wisdom, and madness. It arouses and begets both the soft and the dark parts of our natures. Lovers and thieves, werewolves and witches, medicine men, madmen and midwives—all are children of the moon. In ancient times, the moon was the symbol and power of matriarchy, the rule of women before masculine energy conquered the world.

The moon rules the night and the powers of the night. Her light is not her own, so it is indirect, indistinct, cool, and soft. To see by her light is to see in a mirror, by reflection, so nothing is certain. Distortion is always possible, mistakes are easily made, hard edges are banished, and shadows rule. Because of this, the Moon card in tarot is associated with deceit and delusion.

The souls of the dead are said to reside in the moon, and those same souls are said to descend from the moon to take on new incarnations. All solid realities lose their substance by moonlight, and all shapes as yet unborn wait in the moon's realm for their turn to become fully manifest. Therefore, the moon is said to rule the astral plane, the place of ghosts, spirits, and dreams.

Because of this, the moon is foremost among the celestial sources of magick. All magicians in all times and places have known and used the powers of the moon to perform magickal acts. In tarot, the appearance of the moon may signify a good time to do magick.

We briefly discussed many things about the moon and many others have not even been mentioned because the subject is so large and space is limited. But in all that we've said so far, the moon has been talked about as though it were one thing—one object, recognizable, as most things are, by one appearance.

The fact is, as everyone knows, the moon has many aspects, and she changes, at least a little, every night. She becomes new, waxes, becomes full, wanes, and becomes dark every month. Her changes are endless but perfectly predictable and steady. Because of this she is the symbol of time as a circle. The Wheel of the Year and the seasons, the ebb and flow of the tides of the sea, the menstrual cycle of the whole female gender, the first and most enduring human calendar are all marked and predicted by the rhythmic changes of the moon's face.

For this reason, the moon is a symbol of all that is psychic, of crystal balls, of tarot itself, and of women.

The Moon in Tarot

In the Rider-Waite-Smith tarot deck, the moon appears in: the 2 of Swords, the 7 of Swords, the 8 of Cups, The High Priestess, The Hierophant, The Chariot, and The Moon.

In the 2 and 7 of Swords and The Hierophant, the moon has a purely astrological significance, referring in each case to the astrological attributions of the cards.

> 2 of Swords = Moon in Libra
> 7 of Swords = Moon in Aquarius
> The Hierophant = Taurus (symbol composed of a combination of the sun's disk and the crescent moon)

The High Priestess

The moon in The High Priestess appears in her crown and at her feet. In her crown, it is a general symbol of the divine feminine and refers specifically to her triple role as Maiden, Mother, and Crone (waxing, full, and waning phases). It is also a reference to her esoteric title, Daughter of the Silver Star, and to her connection with the Egyptian goddess Hathor. The sickle moon at her feet is a reference to her other aspect as Christian Mary, the Stella Maris or Star of the Sea, depicted in iconic paintings as riding the boat of the moon across the sea. And of course, the astrological attribution of The High Priestess is the moon.

The Chariot

In The Chariot, the waxing and waning crescent moons on the shoulders of the charioteer are symbols of equipoise, the perfect balance between alternating happiness and sadness, rise and fall, growth and decay.

8 of Cups

The 8 of Cups shows us the sun being eclipsed by the moon. This is a reference to its esoteric title, the Lord of Abandoned Success, with its implication of a necessary journey from light into darkness.

The Moon

In the ultimate moon of tarot, the Moon card itself, it is shown in its disseminating phase just after full. In this phase, astrology tells us that the moon's energy is assimilative, evaluative, and innovative. It is, essentially, a learning moon, appropriate in this card to the experience of the path that lies ahead and to the goal of the mountains in the distance.

• • •

Regardless of the card and regardless of its phase, every appearance of the moon in tarot brings with it the gift of all its meanings and references, ready to the hand of the reader. The third eye is opened, the intuition is primed, and answers to questions arise of themselves.

Astrology, Wicca, Qabalah, alchemy, mythology, psychology, poetry, history, science, and religion all contribute to the staggering quantity of lore about the moon. In the interests of time and sanity, this lesson has to stop here. But if you should become lost in fascination with this subject, you will have, if you wish, a very good life's work ahead of you to learn and understand it all.

STARS

Hello, and welcome to our class on stars. We won't be spending any time on actual stars—not physical ones—in this class. Insofar as physical equals real, we won't be discussing reality. The stars in tarot are entirely symbolic and appear nowhere but in the night sky of the imagination. In fact, not even there, if you're talking about normal imagination. Only in the imagination of esoteric symbol makers do these particular stars exist at all.

But everything that catches and holds our attention in the physical world has its counterpart somewhere in our inner landscape. And it is in this way that the physical universe becomes our teacher.

Before allowing ourselves to be influenced by the filter of the teaching of others, it's a good idea to look inside for our own meanings and interpretations. So for a few minutes, let's do a little stargazing in our own private universes. Let's see what they look like and find out if they mean anything to us personally.

Take a moment to turn off all the artificial light in your surroundings, and to eliminate as much inessential noise as possible.

Take a comfortable position, one that you can maintain without fidgeting for five minutes.

Close your eyes. Breathe and relax.

Surround yourself with darkness and let your thoughts dissolve in that darkness.

Let your emotions drift away into the shadows. Let physical sensations lose all importance, and let every desire fall away beyond remembering. Wrap yourself in peaceful, quiet darkness, and drift.

The darkness becomes your own clear night sky, without moon or cloud. A star appears. Pay attention to it.

You notice that more stars have appeared. Become very much aware of them.

Ask yourself three questions:
    1. What are these stars?
    2. How do I feel about them?
    3. What do they mean to me?

The time has come to return. The stars fade from view, and only the clear darkness of your own inner night remains. Rest peacefully there for a moment.

Become aware of your surroundings. Wiggle your fingers and toes. Take two deep breaths, and when you're ready, open your eyes. Welcome back.

Take a moment to restore some light to your surroundings. Do that now.

Star
Contemplation

97

For the next couple of minutes write down your answers to these questions you asked yourself. When writing down a contemplation, the best method is to write continuously without internal editing until you feel you're finished. Try that now.

Stars as Symbols

There are, as we said earlier, physical, actual, real stars. There are, as you've just discovered, the personal stars of intuitive consciousness. Now we'll talk about stars as symbols. The essence of star symbolism is contained in three words—unreachable, innumerable, and unapproachable. The stars are far beyond our grasp, there are way more of them than we can count, and their power is so great that we cannot get close to them.

When we view them from our natural distance, stars do have natural symbolic importance; we tend to associate them with light, both divine and benign. They are the lights of heaven. In some traditions, every star is an angel, and every human being is said to have one of these angels as a personal mentor and protector.

Most people think of stars as both beautiful and benevolent. They make us feel peaceful and hopeful when we look at or think about them. This is why most readers interpret The Star card in tarot as meaning hope and good fortune.

Because human ambition seems to be limitless, and stars are obviously so far beyond our grasp, they are the target of the most far-flung ambitions of practical and theoretical science. To aim for the stars is a popular description of any great personal aspiration. This element of intense aspiration is always potentially present when a star appears as a symbol. It is the essence of everything desirable and seemingly unreachable.

All this is generally true of stars when we see them against the wide canvas of the sky and when they have no particular shape that catches our attention. But as symbols, they are most often found in other contexts and in very special shapes, and then they are radically different from everything we've just said.

The significance of a star as a symbol depends on its shape. In the esoteric universe, which includes tarot, stars are geometric shapes, regular arrangements of points or rays around a center. The significance of one of these magickal stars depends on how many points or rays it has. Generally, there are five-, six-, seven-, eight-, and nine-pointed stars that represent most of what esoteric tradition has to say about the subject. In the RWS tarot, you will only find five-, six- and eight-pointed stars, so we'll just talk about those. And of course, we'll need to be brief, as usual.

THE PENTAGRAM

The five-pointed star, or pentagram, is the most universally recognized star shape. You'll see it most clearly in the Ace of Pentacles and find it in all the cards of the suit of Pentacles. It appears on the flags of nations all over the world. But more important for our purposes, it is a ubiquitous symbol of magick. In spiritual traditions, it can represent everything from the angelic to the demonic, and it plays a major role in the internal symbolism of esoteric orders like Freemasonry, Rosicrucianism, and the Golden Dawn.

In these orders, as well as in alchemy and Qabalah, the pentagram is most important as the symbol of the microcosm, the world below in the magickal saying, "As above, so below." It is the stylized picture of the human form, with four limbs, a head, and a torso. It is the emblem of the primary Renaissance concept that "man is the measure of all things," and that may well be the absolute foundation statement of all of Western esotericism.

THE HEXAGRAM

The six-pointed star, or hexagram, is also known as the Star of David and the Seal of Solomon. As the Star of David, it is a relatively recent emblem of Judaism in the form of Zionism. As the Seal of Solomon, legend has it that it was engraved on the magickal ring worn by King Solomon and contained the secrets of Solomon's magickal powers.

As you probably know, a hexagram is made of two interlaced triangles, one pointing upward and one downward. One triangle is the symbol of masculine fire and the other is the symbol of feminine water. The whole world is supposed to be made of the interaction of these two principles. The hexagram is the symbol of the macrocosm, the above in "As above, so below."

These things are well known. But there are lots of interesting things that are less well known about this form of the star. Let me give you an example from alchemy.

First, carefully draw a hexagram. Make it of two triangles, each about two inches on a side.

> Above the top point, write "Lead – Saturn."
> Below the bottom point, write "Silver – Moon."
> Label the top left point "Iron – Mars."
> The top right point is "Tin – Jupiter."
> The bottom right point is "Copper – Venus."
> The bottom left point is "Mercury – Mercury."
> In the center of the hexagram, write "Gold – Sun."

Now draw the hexagram again in the same way.

Above the top point of your hexagram write "Fire."
Write "Water" below the bottom point.
In the angle between the two points on the right,
    write "Air."
Between the two points on the left, write "Earth."
Label the top right point of the hexagram "Hot."
Label the top left point "Dry."
Label the bottom left point "Cold."
Label the bottom right point "Wet."

In the Hermetic tradition, the hexagram is a symbol of the Great Work of human evolution. It is the seven metals as the essential quality of all material things, and it is the seven planets as the totality of the heavens. The center is the Sun and Gold, the symbolic state of perfection, surrounded by all less-than-perfect states.

The Great Work of alchemy is the transmutation of all the fragmentary states of human consciousness, represented by the circle of less-than-perfect physical and spiritual qualities. And this is done by manipulating the four elements and their four alchemical properties. All of this is captured neatly by the simple picture of a six-pointed star.

THE EIGHT-POINTED STAR

The eight-pointed star is the star of the spirit. In several traditions, there are seven rungs on a ladder that lead to heaven and a state of human perfection. One way of representing those rungs is as the seven planets of ancient astronomy, called the Wanderers because they are constantly moving. Each of these is a lesson to be learned and a step to be taken in spiritual evolution. When all this is completed, the eighth level of perfection, the level of the fixed and eternal stars of heaven, is reached.

The eight-pointed star is also the symbol of the morning and evening star (actually the planet Venus), said to be the most beautiful of all.

The Stars in Tarot

Let's look at the cards where stars appear: The entire suit of Pentacles, The Devil, The Magician, The Empress, The Hermit, The Fool, The Star, and The Chariot.

In tarot, the pentagram is the central symbol of the whole suit of Pentacles, associated with the element of earth as the final form of the microcosm, or the world of below. It appears in The Devil card in inverted form for two reasons. The first is to symbolize the carnality associated with the Devil by the Church. The second is a reference to the Knights Templar, who were accused of despising the cross as a symbol and worshiping the demon Baphomet, whose symbol was the inverted pentagram. It also appears as one of the suit symbols on the table of The Magician, showing his power over all the elements.

The simple lesson of the pentagram in tarot is contained in one word—earth—and everything associated with it: wealth and possessions, health, and all appetites and sensations.

The hexagram appears in two cards, The Empress and The Hermit. In both cases, the reference is Qabalistic. In The Empress's crown there are twelve stars, representing the entire zodiac said to be embedded in Wisdom, which is the beginning of her emergent path on the Tree of Life. In The Hermit, the hexagram in his lantern is the symbol of the light he creates by

THE EMPRESS.

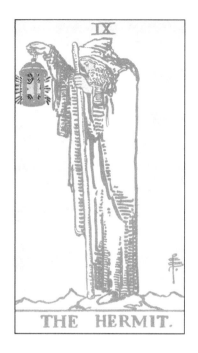

THE HERMIT.

reaching the boundary between the world above and the world below at the top of his mountain. This boundary between above and below is the end of his path of return on the Tree of Life.

The simple lesson of the hexagram is wisdom and light.

The eight-pointed star can be found in The Fool and The Star. In The Fool, the twelve stars on his tunic infuse the perfection of the eight-pointed star into the twelve signs of the zodiac. In The Star card, the entire path of spiritual ascent, represented by the seven lower stars, is completed in the perfect beauty of the eighth star. The Star card

THE FOOL.

THE STAR.

THE CHARIOT.

is called the natural intelligence and represents the perfection at the heart of nature.

The simple lesson of the eight-pointed star is the feeling of beauty and perfection that rewards the completion of an inner journey.

All three kinds of stars are in the canopy of The Chariot, which is a Masonic symbol. In Freemasonry, the starry canopy is the symbol of the whole universe—above and below, inside and outside, mystical and manifest—all of which is considered to be the scope of the work of an initiate. The stars in the canopy are also a reference to the esoteric title of The Chariot, The House of Influence, by which all good things are brought from above to below and from below to above.

The simple lesson of the stars in The Chariot is that they represent the whole universe and all the good things in it.

• • •

As with so many of the visual symbols of tarot, the star deserves a great deal more study and contemplation than we can give it here. Such a study would constitute a worthy journey, and it might well become your own inner journey to complete such a study over time.

POOLS

Hello, and welcome to our class on pools, which appear in three cards—Temperance, The Star, and The Moon. These are natural pools, not constructed or modified by human intervention.

This has been a particularly interesting image to develop into a class. In all the symbol dictionaries that we own, pools are not even mentioned. And in esoteric tarot literature, the references are few and not very helpful in everyday matters. But our instinct about the importance of the natural pool as a symbol remained strong. So, for lack of any detailed authoritative source, we looked inside ourselves to find what we were positive existed, and there, sure enough, was everything we needed. A portion of this class, then, can claim no other authority than intuition.

Our first associations with the image of a pool are pure fun. When we were little, a pool was a place to play, to swim, and to get cool and clean. As we got older, the list of pleasures we associated with natural pools came to include reverie, meditation, and occasional romantic interludes in their peaceful presence. These were real pools and real experiences, not symbols.

The first thing to know about the pool as a symbol is that, like the moon, it is purely feminine. No masculine attributes can be found in it. It is a container made of earth that holds water. Although pools in the physical world may vary, symbolic pools are deep, dark, reflective, and cold. They contain no light, no heat, and no air of their own. Pools are curved or irregular in shape, not straight edged or sharp. They welcome and frighten by turns. They are relatively small and intimate, not at all demanding, grand, or imposing.

A pool may be fresh or stagnant, clear or murky, pure or poisoned. It may be old or newly formed, but the chances are it contains and nurtures life.

The surface of a pool is open and obvious, a place where things can float, suspended between the air and light of the world above and the dark watery world below. Its depths are full of mysteries and secrets and contain both life and death.

Take a moment to see if this description fits your own observations and sensibilities.

Now, the thing about any symbol, especially a purely feminine one, is that it is far better to know it through experience than through talk. You already know that anything in the physical world that catches and holds your attention takes up residence in your consciousness, lives inside you somewhere, whether you are aware of it or not. To enter your inner universe and find whatever you are looking for is a simple matter of technique. In a moment, we'll journey to the pool that exists within us all. This is not a tarot symbol. It is a part of our purely personal landscape, so the pool we discover will be different for each of us.

Take a moment to turn off or dim your lights and get comfortable.

Pool Journey	Close your eyes and surround yourself with darkness.
	Breathe and relax.
	Float for awhile without thought, feeling, or sensation. Drift and rest.
	You find yourself now in a stone room whose proportions are equal and whose shape is that of a cube. The room is square and as high as it is long and wide. The floor is cool, and you notice that your feet are bare.
	The room has a single door and no windows, although there is enough light to see by. Go to the door, open it, and step through.

You find yourself on the landing of a staircase that descends out of sight. Take a minute to observe and remember the landing.

In a moment, you'll begin to descend the staircase.

Do that now.

As you descend step by step, pay attention to what you see and feel.

You reach the bottom of the stairs and find yourself on a narrow beach. You can feel the sand under your feet.

Directly in front of you is a body of water stretching away into the distance. A pier leads from the water's edge to a boat. See this clearly.

Walk across the sand and along the pier to the boat. Go on board and take a minute to explore. Soon, this boat will begin to carry you across the water to an island, on which you will find the pool that awaits you.

The boat moves away from the pier, and you begin your journey. Be completely aware as you travel. Remember everything.

Ahead of you, an island appears. On your next breath, you reach it and step ashore.

Explore the island until you find the pool that is hidden on it. Observe everything. When you reach the pool, sit beside it and rest.

Now, if you wish, but only if you wish, disrobe and enter the pool. You have the ability to descend safely into the depths and experience complete and prolonged immersion.

For the next few minutes, be aware with all your senses and with your thoughts and feelings as well. Explore the waters in any way you wish. Let the experience affect you deeply.

The time has come to emerge from the waters of the pool. Dry and dress if you need to, and then find a good place by the side of the pool to sit and meditate.

Breathe and relax.

You have traveled far and experienced much. Take some time to contemplate what you have seen and felt on your journey.

When you feel ready to return, slowly become aware that you once again inhabit your familiar physical body and the place where your body is physically present. Wiggle your toes. Clench your fingers and relax them.

Take two deep breaths, and, when you're ready, open your eyes but stay in a meditative state.

Welcome back!

Take a moment to restore some light to your surroundings.

For the next few minutes, remember your experiences clearly and write down the most important parts of your journey. Pay special attention to your experience of the pool.

• • •

Everything that you observed and experienced is personal, and it exists within you to revisit whenever you wish. Your own awareness is the basin, and your journey is the water of the pool within you. Be aware that your journey is another name for the totality of your life experience. In this way, your physical body and the experience of life that animates it together form a great and mysterious pool.

The Pools in Tarot

In tarot, the pool has more specialized meanings, depending upon where you find it. These meanings are esoteric and concern themselves with the ceremonial magician's spiritual odyssey. Each pool is found in the landscape of a successively more elevated path on the Tree of Life. The pool in The Moon is the darkest and most melancholy. In The Star, the waters of the pool are much lighter and cleaner and represent an advance in personal evolution. The pool in Temperance is water at its clearest and coldest and is a big step upward and onward.

The Moon

The meaning of the pool in The Moon is relatively simple. The Moon card as a whole shows the first steps of personal evolution for the awakened spirit and the long path that lies ahead. The pool is the darkness of the dream of the personality asleep in the physical world. From the perspective of Ceremonial Magick, everyday life and all its concerns are considered to be the dark water and mud at the bottom of this pool. The crayfish is the primitive consciousness that rises out of the darkness of the water below into the light of the moon above to begin its long spiritual journey.

The Star

Here, too, the meaning of the pool is simple. It is the great pool of spiritual awareness that we explore by meditation in the hope of discovering our own innate perfection. The Star is called the natural intelligence, and it is understood that by traveling on this path of the Tree of Life, all of nature, including our own, can be perfected. But, of course, meditation requires effort, discipline, will, and desire. According to the magickal dictum that "man is the measure of all things," the message of the pool in The Star card is that the perfection of nature itself depends on the exercise of all these qualities in ourselves.

Temperance

To understand the pool in Temperance, you need
to know that it is half of a more complex symbol
that is part Qabalah and part alchemy. This symbol is one of spiritual sexuality, a kind of Hermetic
tantra, that invokes both masculine and feminine
energies, but only in one person at a time.

   You will notice, if you look carefully at the card,
that on the forehead of the Archangel Michael
(the main figure in the foreground) there is a sun
disk, a circle with a point in its center. The pool
is at the bottom of the card, underneath his foot.
The pool and the sun disk refer to the two ends of
the path of Temperance on the Tree of Life—the
lunar pool of Yesod below and the solar disk of
Tiphereth above.

   The pool is the element of water and a symbol of pure feminine
sexuality. The sun is the element of fire and a symbol of pure masculine sexuality. They exist together in every human being, both separated and connected by the path of Temperance on the Tree of Life.

   It is said that by a kind of alchemical-spiritual masturbation,
the pool and the sun, the water and the fire, the feminine and the
masculine, are united in a vast vibratory orgasm that propels the
seeker out of the physical state and into the spiritual one. This is
the crucial breakthrough on the path of spiritual elevation, and it
can only be achieved by using the rocket booster of sexual magick.
If this fails, the seeker reaches his or her limit in the experience of
The Tower. This is an interesting concept that needs a lot more
explanation than we can give it here. By the way, the two cups that
Michael is using to pour energy back and forth are a symbol of solitary sexual energy manipulation.

The thing to remember about the pool as a symbol is that it is a picture of ordinary life as the starting point for spiritual adventure and personal evolution. It can also be useful to remember the pool as a simple, pleasant, and beautiful part of nature.

Reading Practice

As you can see, in tarot, the pool in every case is the official symbol of the beginning of a stage of personal evolution and elevation. This can be difficult to apply to the situations of everyday life, but it can done. Our suggestion is that in a reading you take what is useful in this symbolism and modify it to reflect the needs of the moment. When it's appropriate, or if you prefer, you can work with your own purely personal associations for the pool instead.

One good way to learn how to do that is to put the symbolism of the pool in the context of some actual readings. Here are questions from three hypothetical querents for you to answer that will help to root the information and ideas in this lesson in actual practice.

Personal Reading Style Evaluation

QUESTION #1: *I'm a twenty-four-year old Iraq war veteran who is suffering severe post-traumatic stress disorder. I'm feeling lost, angry, depressed, and melancholy. The world seems like an awful place even when I watch kids playing ball outside my window. I can't connect with anybody, and I feel mean and violent a lot of times. Even with therapy and the support of my family who love me, I don't know what I should do. I came to you for a reading because I thought, "Who knows? Maybe the cards can help."*

You decide to do a one-card reading and you draw The Moon.

What does the pool in the card tell you that can be helpful?

QUESTION #2: *I am a forty-seven-year old woman with a boring husband, two nice children, a career of my own, and a thoroughly respectable life. I've fallen in love with my parish priest. My question is, "What now?"*

You draw The Star for a one-card reading.
What answer does the card, and specifically the pool in the card, have for your querent?

QUESTION #3: *I am a sixteen-year old girl, and there's two really great guys who say they love me. One is sweet and handsome and writes poetry and has the softest touch, and the other is strong and has a great body and does sports and is very exciting and fun to be with. They don't know about each other, and when I'm with one I feel like I'm cheating on the other, but I can't give either one up. Is this wrong? I don't know what to do.*

You draw Temperance for a one-card reading.
What's your advice, based on the card in general and the pool in particular?

• • •

These are intentionally complex and difficult questions to answer, but people often face such situations in their lives. The value of tarot is that it can always be counted on to give a useful perspective in any situation.

INTEGRATION:
MOONS, STARS, AND POOLS

Hello, and welcome to our integration class for moons, stars, and pools. These images appear in:

Ace of Pentacles
2 of Swords
7 of Swords
8 of Cups
The Fool
The Magician
The High Priestess
The Empress
The Hierophant
The Chariot
The Hermit
Temperance
The Devil
The Star
The Moon

Normally, when we do an integration class, we begin with a reminder of the general sense of the images we have discussed. Then we do a brief recapitulation of the specific meanings of those images as they appear in different cards. We do this to help you remember the large amount of information we've covered in the last three classes.

This time, we're going to approach the task of remembering and integration in a different way. Instead of hearing the information again, you're going to find out how much you remember without prompting. And then you'll have a chance to see if you can put what you've learned to use. We'll do all this in the simplest way—with questions.

Before we begin with the questions themselves, it's a good idea to point out that there is more than one kind and style of question one can ask about tarot meanings and symbols. Everyone is different and tends to be interested in and active on different levels, so the questions also tend to be on different levels.

There are practical questions whose concern is everyday life. There are psychological and emotional questions that deal with very personal and internal things. Some people are fascinated with the esoteric and occult, and some have a tendency to be in love with broad philosophical and spiritual issues.

The fact is, every tarot card and every image and symbol speaks to all of these kinds of questions simultaneously. So your job in this lesson is to remember, understand, and use what you have learned in a way that suits and interests you. It's useful to remember, though, that querents also differ in personal style, so you will want to be fluent in as many styles and on as many levels as you can absorb.

The first questions for you to answer, then, are:

What level and style of issue is most comfortable for you?

What kind of question do you answer best:

- practical and useful
- emotional and psychological
- spiritual and philosophical
- esoteric and abstract

*Reading
Practice*

Can you work comfortably in more than one of these areas?

Is there one or more area that is definitely not your cup of tea?

It's useful to be quite clear on your predilections and strengths, and to know where you are not strong or comfortable.

Since our most recent classes were on moons, stars, and pools, the next question is:

What do you remember about the general issues of:
- moons
- stars
- pools

Then ask:
What specific meanings do these images have when they appear in different cards?

Finally, ask:
How and in what context is this information useful to you as a person and as a reader?

Clear and complete answers to these questions will tell you what you've learned, even if the answer sometimes is "I don't know." You can use these questions, or variations on them, to measure your progress in grasping, remembering, and integrating the material of this course as it continues to unfold in classes to come.

Before we get together again, take some time to ask and answer these questions for all the images we've studied in this course so far. You will find the process very helpful and very revealing.

SYMBOL SPREAD:
THE POOL, MOON, AND STAR

This spread is based upon the symbols studied in our classes on pools, moons, and stars. It makes use of four cards, and although it is subtle, this is a strong spread and is particularly good for manifesting your dream or achieving an ambition. It is not a step-by-step instruction manual, but rather it should be considered a guide to some of the broader issues or considerations involved.

The concept of this spread is a pool, which shows a shimmering surface as well as the depth of the water below. In the sky above, you see the moon and a bright star.

Positions #1 and #2 compose the pool, #3 is the moon, and #4 is the star. Please note that these are position names—not to be confused with the cards of The Moon and The Star. The positions should be filled with whichever cards are drawn.

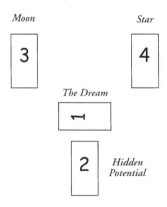

Position #1, the Dream card, is placed horizontally and is read as if upright.

Position #2, the Hidden Potential card, is placed vertically beneath the Dream.

Position #3, the Moon, appears above the pool to the left.
Position #4, the Star, appears above the pool to the right.

The Dream

This horizontal card represents the shimmering surface of a pool, which reflects the object of your desire. This may be something you wish to have, be, or do. The card in this position will show you an aspect of your dream that you can already envision. You may approach this reading with something already in mind, or let the card suggest a dream for you to consider. It should always be read as if upright.

Hidden Potential

Below the surface of the pool are things you cannot see. The deep water contains your hidden potential—the matrix that forms the substance of your dream. You can think of it as a secret ingredient to your recipe for success. An upright card in this position is close to the surface and indicates that its energy can be used as soon as you are ready to make a commitment to your dream. A reversed card is deeper down and may indicate that you'll have to work a little harder to access this energy or that your dream requires a greater risk than you might think. This does not necessarily mean that you should abandon your dream—just that you'll have to dive a little deeper to find what you need.

Moon

As the moon in the sky is constantly cycling through its phases, the card in this position represents something that must change.

This could be a plan of action, timing, or an attitude shift. Read the card's upright or reversed orientation as you would in any reading to gain some insight into the nature of this change.

Star

The Star position, on the other hand, represents a stable force— what stays the same. If you have already been working to realize your dream, this card will tell you something you should keep on doing. If this is a new dream, it will describe the way in which you should remain steady. As before, consider the orientation of the card as you normally would.

• • •

The Pool, Moon, and Star spread can be read quickly, but it is best done in a state of quiet contemplation, as if you were sitting by the edge of a pool under a beautiful night sky.

4

HORSES, SUNS, BANNERS

HORSES

Hello, and welcome to our class on horses in tarot. In the Rider-Waite-Smith deck, horses appear in seven cards—the four Knights, Death, The Sun, and the 6 of Wands. In other decks, they can be found in other cards as well, most often in The Chariot.

Wherever you find the image of a horse as a symbol, you find beauty, speed, power, nobility, and underlying all, freedom and a sense of distance. The horse as a symbol is magnificent.

Now, right now, before we say any more . . .

The Journey of the Horse

Close your eyes. Breathe and relax. Surround yourself with darkness and rest.

In a moment, a doorway will open in that darkness, and you will emerge into an unknown, wild, and endless landscape. This will happen on your next breath.

Look down at your feet. You will not be surprised to find that you have four of them, all hooved. You have the form, the heart, the spirit of a horse. Become aware of yourself and the form you have taken. Take a minute to know the kind of horse that you are.

Ahead of you lies the unknown. Enter it in your new form. Do there what you should do, go where you must go, and become what you must become. Only about fifteen minutes will pass according to the clock, but when you come back, you will have spent an eternal moment in another world as a another being.

The time has come to return. Take a moment to say a proper farewell to the landscape of the horse. When you have done so, find your way back to the doorway by which you arrived.

Soon you will step back through the portal between the worlds. When you do so, you will once again acquire your human form, and you will rest in the darkness that surrounds you. This will happen on your next breath.

Become aware now of your normal environment. Wiggle your fingers and toes. Lightly stamp the ground or the floor beneath your feet three times. Take two deep breaths, and when you are ready, open your eyes.

Now take some time to record the essence and most important parts of your experience on paper.

• • •

The horse is a part of symbol, myth, and legend across the face of the earth. Although it came later to some places than others, whenever and wherever the horse appeared, it entered the life and mythology of humanity in a deep and immediate way. Always, the horse became a god or goddess, or was said to be the child of a god or goddess, and was associated simultaneously with the underworld and with the heavens.

From being its own wild, free, and beautiful creature, it became a servant of the gods in myth and of humanity on earth. It earned its way by pulling or carrying—chariots, carriages, wagons, and riders both human and divine. Horses pulled the chariot of the sun across the sky, carried divine and human warriors into battle, transported princesses to their royal weddings, and carried kings and emperors in procession. Conquerors on horseback swept across continents; jockeys to this day sweep around tracks in the quintessential human activity of the race. Horses have always been the treasured possessions and companions of hunters and travelers everywhere. And they were honored as the most valuable of sacrifices to the gods when sacrifice was needed.

Horses are so much a part of human history and all its stories that they seem indispensable to, even inseparable from, humanity. Out of this intimacy, the myth of the centaur—half man and half horse—was born. In fact, the stories, myths, legends, and historical importance of horses are so manifold and so universal that they overburden the possibility of telling in such a short space as this lesson.

For our purposes, it is enough to describe their symbolism in tarot. But description will be kept short, just enough to act as a springboard for experience. We have already had one experience of the horse, and there will be more before we're done. This is a symbol that gains more from being and doing than from telling.

In the seven cards that contain a horse, three are lunar horses, two are solar, and two are terrestrial.

First in Asia, and later in Greece, the Middle East, and Europe, legend had it that the horse was created by the gods of earth and water. Horses arose from the depths, roamed the night, and were ruled by the moon. In time, the gods of air and sun laid claim to them as well. And horses carried the divinities and heroes of both above and below wherever they wished to go.

But always, the horse is said to have a special affinity with the underworld and the souls of the dead. Dead souls know nothing of the landscape of that underworld, and horses, who know it intimately, are their guides. Heroes who guide their horses into and out of earthly adventures, reverse their roles when they need to enter the world of shades and shadows. Horses know the way and know the dangers, and they lead the heroes into and out of the realms of darkness.

Death

The horse in the Death card of tarot is such a guide. It is the horse who chooses the path and the pace, and Death is content to go where he is taken. Here, the horse is pale, ghostly, a being of the moon, of the night, and the underworld, although he is pictured as white in a clearly lit landscape.

There are two keys to this picture: One is the sun, simultaneously setting and rising in the background, establishing the time as being between dusk and dawn. The other is the cliff, which establishes a landscape of life above and death below, with the horse, Death, and all the human figures in the underworld below.

Knight of Cups

The second lunar horse is found in the Knight of Cups, who travels on the mythic journey of the seeker of the grail. He is an adventurer who has brought his horse to the river that separates ordinary reality from the perilous and sacred landscape of the heart. From this point on, it is the horse who will guide the rider.

Knight of Pentacles

In the imagery of the Knight of Pentacles the horse is black, the symbolic color of the earth from which it arose. It is already in its element here. It is standing still because it has arrived where it is supposed to be. It has brought the knight to the end of his journey. The journey of emergence is complete, and the journey of return awaits its beginning. To survive the journey of return, the Knight of Pentacles must remain surrendered to the power, the knowledge, and the will of his horse.

Knight of Swords

Here, the horse is truly white, a terrestrial being whose color is the color of purity, beauty, and nobility—qualities which he transmits to his rider. These qualities transform the Knight of Swords from a brute, a bully, and a killer into a warrior and a hero.

Knight of Wands

The red horse of the Knight of Wands is a solar horse, whose quality is fire. As with the horse of the Knight of Swords, he imbues his rider with virtues, the godlike qualities of immediacy, certainty, fearlessness, and invulnerability.

6 of Wands

Here again, we have the white terrestrial horse that carries his rider from the past into the present and toward the future in the world of human events. Because the intent of this card is to picture victory, the horse is white to symbolize nobility, triumph, and the mildness of perfect surrender to the rider's will.

The Sun

This is the quintessential solar horse, steed of the gods, worthy mount of the ultimate rider. Horse and rider are equal in virtue, purity, and nobility. Both are without blemish, perfect within and without, and they are in perfect harmony of direction and intent.

• • •

These are the seven horses of tarot.

The Journey of the Horse and Rider

We're about to begin another journey.

Begin by spending two minutes carefully examining and memorizing the landscapes of the seven cards with horses, so that you can see them in detail when you close your eyes.

Now close your eyes and see each landscape in your mind in vivid detail.

Open your eyes and look at the cards again. Remember everything.

At this point, take a moment to dim or extinguish the lights in your surroundings.

Close your eyes once again. Surround yourself with darkness and rest.

Once again, a doorway opens onto a landscape you do not know. You will enter that landscape on your next breath.

You are a rider now, on one of the seven horses of tarot in the landscape of your chosen mount. Go forth into that landscape and guide or be guided by your horse to whatever awaits you there.

It is time to return from whence you came. When you are done, return to the doorway between the worlds and wait. In a moment, you will dismount, move through the doorway into darkness, and rest. This will happen on your next breath.

Become aware of your surroundings. Clench your fingers and toes, then relax them.

Take two deep breaths, and when you are ready, open your eyes.

Welcome back. Now take the time to record your experiences.

• • •

When a horse catches your attention in a reading, let it remind you that it is a symbol of the energy and style of a journey. Sometimes the journey is lunar and connected with the night, what a Jungian would call your shadow. Sometimes it is solar and connected with light and spirit. And sometimes it's terrestrial and concerned with adventures in daily life.

• The pale horse of Death takes you through your own world of shades and shadows.

• The horse of the Knight of Cups carries you across the river that separates the sacred from the ordinary, into the world of the heart.

• The Knight of Pentacles sits astride the black horse of the earth, at the end of one journey and the beginning of another.

• The heroic Knight of Swords rides his magnificent steed toward a glorious adventure.

• The red horse of the Knight of Wands is ready to go wherever and whenever the spirit demands.

• The mild and noble white horse in the 6 of Wands carries the worthy hero high above the crowd in a moment of glory.

• The pure, perfect beauty of the white horse of The Sun carries its radiant rider forward to fulfill a happy destiny.

In tarot, horse and rider are inseparable. The horse gives its rider its virtues and the power to move forward. The rider gives the horse direction and purpose. Together, they are always the central figures of a story—of a significant story or important chapter in the life of whoever comes to tarot for a reading.

SUNS

Hello, and welcome to our class on the suns of tarot. Suns appear in seven cards—The Fool, The Hierophant, The Lovers, The Chariot, Death, Temperance, and The Sun.

Suns, like moons and stars, change their meanings, references, and significance from card to card. You may remember from earlier classes that moons differ by their phases and stars by the number of their points or rays. For suns, the difference is found in what sky or heaven they appear in.

There is an alchemical sun, a Qabalistic sun, a Masonic sun, an Egyptian sun, an astrological sun, a mythological sun, a psychological sun, and a scientific sun—all forms of what the mind makes of the observable sun in the sky.

Each of these suns is fascinating in its own right. Each sheds light on ourselves and the world we live in. All of these suns are a large part of the answer to the questions of who we are and where we come from. We have only a few pages to look at these suns, and because space is limited, we will not be blinded by what we see. However, if we had unlimited pages, what there is to see would be dazzling.

To mention moons and stars here is useful as a contrast, a background of difference against which suns can be measured. Moons and stars are fully defined by what they are: objects in the night sky. As objects, their significance ranges from that of physical bodies to that of spiritual entities, even deities. But whatever they are, they are.

Suns, however, although they are symbolic and physical objects, are also powers and sources of power. You could go so far as to say that they are the source of all the power there is.

If you live physically, the sun is the ultimate source of your life's energy and being.

If you live psychologically, the sun's power is the source and nature of your awareness.

If you have a spiritual life, the sun is the radiant source and nature of your spirit. If anything, including yourself, exists at all in any form, it is the sun from which it springs and by whose power it continues.

Were the sun on any level of being to be extinguished, all life and being on that level would be extinguished with it. This cannot be said of any other phenomenon in all the many worlds. So the one thing you will want to remember about suns among all the things that we discuss in this lesson is that the sun is power.

For a moment, contemplate this statement. The sun is power. Can you validate that statement from your own experience, or do you question it?

Now let's take some time to look at the sun through several different pairs of eyes.

Astrology

The sun of astrology is one planet among several that revolve around the center of personal consciousness. In modern times, although it may once have been different, the influence of the sun is in what is most visible of the individual it describes. In broad strokes, it shows what can be seen of a person on and close to the surface and what will influence that person's life in the most direct and immediate way. The symbol for the sun in astrology is a circle with a point in the center.

Freemasonry

In Freemasonry, the sun is half of the entire manifest universe. It is paired with the combination of moon and stars.

The sun is the daylight half of things and symbol of all that can be associated with daylight. The composite symbol of moon and stars is the nighttime half of things and all that can be associated with the night. The sun and the moon and stars always appear together, never separately, since the whole manifest world is made up of both together. They are the basic reciprocal duality, and neither can exist without the other.

In Freemasonry, the symbol of the sun is most often a full-faced disk with emanating rays that is called a sunburst. But when a simple, abbreviated symbol is required, that symbol is a circle with a point in the center.

Alchemy

The evolution of both matter and spirit, from its lowest to its highest state, is the ultimate task and imperative of alchemy. That evolution is sometimes described as a series of stages, like the rungs on a ladder that must be ascended step by step. Each stage in this progression is a refinement and improvement on what went before, and each is given a planetary name and a metal to go with it. The planet is the sphere of a Greek god with lessons to teach and powers to bestow. The metal associated with the planet is the material equivalent of the psychological and spiritual nature of the planetary sphere.

For alchemy, the sun is the purest, most perfect, and most powerful step on the ladder of evolution. Its metal is gold, the purest and most refined of metals and the perfection of nature. In alchemy, the symbol for the sun and also for gold is a circle with a dot in the middle.

Qabalah

The sun appears three times in Qabalah, but never directly.

Its first appearance is as the Crown, the number one on the Tree of Life. It is the scintillating beginning of all creation and contains within its abstract glory all that is to follow. Its color is white.

Second, it is Beauty, the number six at the center of the Tree of Life. This is the sun whose radiance permeates and defines the world of the spirit and is both the source and the goal of spiritual enlightenment. Its color is yellow.

Third, it is the thirtieth path on the Tree of Life, the Hebrew letter Resh, which means beginning and is associated with consciousness in the world of nature. It is the light in the eyes of living beings that signifies awareness, and its color is red-orange.

Qabalah has little tolerance for pictures or visual imagery, so it has no graphic sign for the sun.

Science

Science sees the sun as the center of our immediate universe and the source of all energy, and hence of all life, in the solar system of which the earth is a part. The sun is a star, and stars are a coalescence of the matter and energy of the entire universe and the big bang that gave rise to it all. We are said to be made of star stuff, and the sun is our personal star. With it we live. Without it we do not.

In astronomy, the science of planets, sun, and stars, the symbol for the sun is a circle with a dot in the center.

Egypt

A very long time ago, the Egyptians saw the sun rise each morning from the underworld and depart the sky for that same underworld each evening. The night was seen to surround both the worlds of the living and the dead, the worlds above and below. Day was seen to be a periodic brightness drawn on the canvas of perpetual night. The sun was the child of Hathor, creator of the world and goddess of the night. Each new day was a rebirth; with each new dawn the sun was reborn from the womb of Hathor, and the world was renewed as well.

Without the sun, only the gods and goddesses existed. With the birth of the sun, humanity and all mortal beings could exist as well.

In the hieroglyphics of ancient Egypt, the symbol for the sun was a circle with a dot in the middle, the seed of life carried in the womb of the goddess. This is the first known appearance of the pointed circle as the symbol of the sun.

Now let's look at the sun in the cards.

The Fool

The sun in The Fool is the Qabalistic sun of the number one, called the Crown. It is the source of what is called the Scintillating Intelligence, which is associated with the path of The Fool. From its sparkle will be made the whole universe that is yet to be born.

It shows fourteen rays, which refer to the numbers one, two, and eleven—numbers one and two on the Tree of Life, called the Crown and Wisdom, and path number 11, called The Fool, which connects them. 1 + 2 + 11 = 14.

The importance of the sun in The Fool is that it is the very beginning of absolutely everything.

The Hierophant

In The Hierophant, the sun is both a Masonic and an astrological symbol. Together with the crescent of the moon, it forms the sign for Taurus (♉), the astrological attribution of The Hierophant. It is a reminder that The Hierophant knows and regulates the secrets of both the light and the dark halves of everything.

The Chariot

The Chariot has the sun in the crown of the charioteer, whose symbolism is also Masonic, including
sun, moon, and stars. The issue of this symbolism
in The Chariot is maintaining internal balance,
staying steady, centered, and effective between the
alternating influences of day and night.

In both The Hierophant and The Chariot, the
sun is a reminder of the duality of celestial symbolism and the necessity to honor the powers of both
day and night in ourselves.

The Lovers

The sun in The Lovers is pure Qabalah, though it
also accords well with Freemasonry. Everything
that was unified in the upper reaches of the Tree
of Life becomes openly divided into pairs of polar
opposites on the path of The Lovers. From this
point onward in the creative process, nothing can
be seen or understood without reference to its
opposite. There is no light without darkness, no
love without hate, no good without evil.

All the pairs of opposites are symbolized by the
man and the woman in the picture. But the uni-
fying angel between them shows the way to bring
opposites together, and the sun behind the angel is

the glory of the middle way from which all opposites emerge and to which, in time, they will all return.

This sun has forty-five rays, referring to the numerical value of the name of Adam in Hebrew. In Adam, male and female were originally united and will eventually be reunited. The sun reminds you that both sides of every issue need each other and that every apparently irreconcilable argument has a resolution.

Death

Then comes Death. In Death, it is not immediately clear from the picture whether the sun in rising or setting, whether we are seeing the hopeful signs of a dawning day or the unavoidable onset of night. Of course, the answer is a bit of both. As the sun rises in one place, it sets in another. Whatever it is doing now, it will eventually do the opposite.

Strictly as a symbol of Death, understood in the usual way as an ending, the sun is setting, and the time is between sunset and dawn. But Death is also a precursor to, and necessary preparation for, renewed life. Understood in this way, the sun is rising and the time is dawn. In Qabalah every path, including Death, is a two-way street.

The symbol of the sun in the Qabalistic view of Death, shows Death as a path that must constantly be traveled in both directions. This is in accord with the Egyptian view of the sun as a deity that travels daily through both the land of the living and the land of the dead.

The sun in Death is there to remind you that every moment is both a beginning and an ending. Which of these you experience at any given moment is a matter of perspective.

Temperance

The sun in Temperance is the sun disk on the angel's forehead. It is a reference to the spiritual sun of Beauty, the number six on the Tree of Life, which is one end of the path of Temperance. It is the fiery half of the extremes of hot and cold that must be experienced on this path to find the precarious balance of the middle way, which is the true lesson of Temperance.

The other half, the extreme of cold, can be found in the water of the lunar pool of nature beneath the angel's feet, which is the other end of the path of Temperance.

Here again, Qabalah and Freemasonry join to express the necessary duality of sun and moon, hot and cold, light and dark. The lesson of the sun here is once again that it is only half of all there is. The other half is night and darkness, and it is just as necessary. This lesson is repeated over and over in tarot, but it is a hard lesson to learn when life is troubling.

The Sun

Finally, the sun makes an appearance as itself in The Sun card. Here it is unequivocally bright and fortunate, without a trace of darkness anywhere. It is the mythological deity of a hundred pantheons, the brilliant ball of fire in the sky drawn by the horses of the gods.

There is one possible source of trouble to be found here if you wish to find it. It is located in the card's esoteric function, which is the double one of Fertility and Barrenness. The unblinking, unshielded sun can burn, blind, and wither what remains too long unprotected from its intensity.

This sun has twenty-two rays, although one is hidden at the top of the card behind the number. There are eleven straight and eleven wavy rays representing the twenty-two paths of the Tree of Life and the twenty-two Major Arcana connected with them. The alternating wavy and straight rays signify the alternation of male and female energies, even in the straightforward brilliance of the sun's unshaded light.

The sun's final lesson in its last appearance in tarot is the pure, unadulterated power that we spoke of at the beginning of this class. It never fades or fails. It plays no favorites. It sees everything, judges nothing, and is equally available to all that exists beneath it.

The power to live, to be, and to act is in infinite supply and is universally available. The power of The Sun does not die with death or fade with night. It is always steady, strong, and certain. It blazes inside of you as well as outside of you, and nothing in the world can extinguish it.

Sun
Meditation
Close your eyes now; breathe and relax. Reflect on the final lesson of the sun. See if you can find the sun blazing within you. If you can, dwell in that experience for a moment. Remember it so you can take it with you.

Take two deep breaths and, when you're ready, open your eyes.

BANNERS

Hello, and welcome to our class on banners, which appear in three cards—Death, The Sun, and Judgement. Banners appear in several Minor Arcana cards as well, but the implications of these banners will be covered in the general discussion.

Imagery in tarot is of three kinds: natural phenomena that have been invested with symbolic significance, objects made by human hands for ordinary purposes but that come to have symbolic meaning, and objects conceived and made for no other purpose than to act as symbols.

Banners are symbols of the third kind. They are very old, probably older than writing or anything resembling civilization.

The essential banner is made of two parts, very like a cross. One part is the vertical, the other the horizontal. The vertical is a rigid pole, whose purpose is to support the horizontal and to raise it above eye level. The pole can be held in the hand, stuck in the ground, or affixed to a high place like a roof or tower. The horizontal is a flexible medium attached to the pole that bears a symbol and unfurls and flies on the wind where everyone can see it.

The purpose of a banner is to make a symbolic statement that can't be missed or ignored. The rigidity and height of the pole give it stature, and the energy of the wind gives it numinous intensity and power. When we speak of a banner, the vertical is implied and generic, but the horizontal is specific and carries all the meaning.

Once upon a time, before humanity could write, banners were made of animal tails or pelts. Their message was simple. The person or group for whom the banner was carried had the qualities of the animal whose skin was attached to the pole.

Eventually, banners were made of leather or cloth and painted with symbols, but their message was the same. They proclaimed the identity, the qualities, and the importance of a person or a group.

In this way, a banner is like a totem. It is so imbued with the significance and importance of a particular identity that it has a power of its own. The presence of a banner on a battlefield, on parade, or on display is the symbol of a living, vital presence. To capture, desecrate, or destroy a banner is to insult and even to injure the reality it represents.

When your banner is flying high above the ground, all is well. When it falls, woe betide you.

It would be fair to say that every human community with a public presence and a sense of its own importance has a banner or a flag, which is a form of banner. Countries and political organizations; religions and spiritual organizations; civic, social, sports, and military groups; even esoteric and magickal orders—all have their banners, and for all, the banners serve the same purpose. They catch the eye, collect and focus the energy, dominate the attention, and unify and imbue with identity a crowd or a group of individuals.

Banners make an impact—they catch the eye and hold it, in tarot as much as anywhere else. But in tarot, as elsewhere, the symbolism and identity displayed on a banner is often enigmatic. You won't grasp it or be compelled by it unless you have been taught beforehand what it means.

Banners appear in tarot directly and indirectly, and their meanings come from two sources: Freemasonry and the Order of the Golden Dawn.

Freemasonry makes liberal use of banners. There are separate ones for the York and Scottish Rites and the Royal Arch Degree, for each of the major officers in a lodge and for each Grand Lodge, as well as for specific rituals and for Freemasonry as a whole. For the Golden Dawn, banners play a similar role and even share some of the symbolic imagery.

The impact of Masonry on banners in tarot may very well come as something of a surprise. Masonic symbolism is largely drawn from biblical sources, especially with regard to King Solomon, around whose temple much of Masonic legend, belief, and practice revolve. The key to the indirect presence of Masonic banner symbolism in tarot can be found in the general standard (or banner) of Freemasonry. Here is a description of its symbolic content.

On the tracing board of the Royal Arch Degree are the banners of the twelve tribes of Israel. These are:

Judah—scarlet, a lion couchant

Issachar—blue, a donkey crouching beneath its burden

Zebulon—purple, a ship

Reuben—red, a man

Simeon—yellow, a sword

Gad—white, a troop of horsemen

Ephraim—green, an ox

Manasseh—flesh colored, a vine by the side of a wall

Benjamin—green, a wolf

Dan—green, an eagle

Asher—purple, a cup

Naphtali—blue, a deer

Four of these banners make the primary symbolism of the general standard of Freemasonry, the banner of the order, which can be carried in all processions of the Craft to distinguish them from any other association or group.

On a shield, divided by a green and yellow cross into four quarters, the following devices can be found:

> In the first quarter is a golden lion on a blue shield to represent the banner of the tribe of Judah.

> In the second quarter is a black ox on a field of gold, which represents the banner of the tribe of Ephraim.

> In the third quarter is a man on a field of gold, which represents the banner of the tribe of Reuben.

> In the fourth quarter is a golden eagle on a blue ground, which represents the banner of the tribe of Dan.

Over the entire shield is the Ark of the Covenant as a crest and underneath is the motto "Holiness to the Lord."

Each of the four symbols in the shield is said to be the banner of one of the four principal tribes of Israel. When the twelve tribes marched through the wilderness of Sinai, they encamped around these four principal banners. On the east were three tribes under the standard of Judah, on the west were three tribes under the standard of Ephraim, on the south were three tribes under the standard of Reuben, and on the north were three tribes under the standard of Dan. The banner of Judah was a lion, that of Ephraim an ox, that of Reuben a man, and that of Dan an eagle.

The banner of Freemasonry is thus made up of and derived from the banners of the four leading tribes of Israel. The simple significance of each symbol is as follows:

The man signifies reason.

The lion is power.

The ox is patience.

The eagle is wisdom.

The Masonic standard is intended to indicate the origin of the Craft from Solomon, the last king of Israel, under whom the twelve tribes were united.

And these four symbols of the Masonic banner appear where in tarot? I'm sure you know where to find them, but did you know what you were looking at?

Now let's look at the three cards in which specific banners appear and talk about their meanings.

Death

First is the black and white banner carried by the skeletal horseman in Death. This is the blaze of the sun in underworld of the dead, pictured as an unfolded white rose on a ground of darkness. The perfection symbolized by the sun as a sunburst in the land of the living takes the form of a five-petaled rose in the land of the dead. Its visible pistils and stamens are a promise of rebirth, a pledge that death is not the end but a beginning.

The Sun

The banner of The Sun card is the red-orange color of the Qabalistic sun in the world of nature, and it is also the color of the thirtieth path on the Tree of Life, which is associated with The Sun. Its shape is a double symbol: first, as the shape of the Egyptian hieroglyph that means Ra, the one god, the god of the sun; second, as the shape of the Hebrew letter Resh, which means beginning or source and is attributed to the thirtieth path on the Tree of Life and The Sun card in tarot. In both cases, the banner shape is suggestive rather than exact.

Judgement

The red cross on a white field of the banner in the Judgement card also has two references. The first is to the banner of the Knights Templar, which was a red cross on a white field. The sworn and primary duty of the Templars was to protect pilgrims as they crossed the borders between the countries and kingdoms of Europe and Asia Minor that lay on the path to the Holy Land. Here, in the card, the boundary is between the dreaming and waking state of the spirit as it rises to heed the call of Gabriel's trumpet.

The second reference is to Mars, whose first duty, similar to that of the Templars, was to guard the innermost and holiest sanctum of a Greek temple, called the adytum.

The visual reference to Mars in the banner is by way of the magic square of Mars, which is five by five. The cross divides the banner into four white corners. The proportion of the corners to the stripe of the cross is two to one. Each corner is said to be made of four small squares; each arm of the cross is said to be made of two small squares of the same size, and the center of the cross is made of one similar square. Four corners of four squares each equals sixteen squares. Four arms made of two squares each, plus one center square equals nine squares. All together, the banner is made of twenty-five squares—five by five, the magic square of Mars.

• • •

The banner of Death focuses your attention on the promise of rebirth and the beginning that follows each ending.

The banner of The Sun reminds you that the sun is the beginning and the source of power of everything in the natural world.

The banner of Judgement is the pledge of protection for every spirit that begins the journey to enlightenment.

Banner Exercise

It is the nature of a banner to focus, inspire, empower, and lead and to do this with a single simple gesture—unfurling a symbol for all to see. The experiential exercise for this class is equally simple—just create a symbol that expresses your identity, focuses your attention, and inspires you to action. This is your personal symbol for your own banner.

You might not immediately create something definitive, but continue working on it until you have succeeded to your own satisfaction. I promise you that your effort will be well rewarded.

Draw your banner here.

INTEGRATION:
HORSES, SUNS, AND BANNERS

Hello, and welcome to our integration class for horses, suns, and banners. These symbols can be found in thirteen cards:

> The four Knights
> The 6 of Wands
> The Fool
> The Hierophant
> The Lovers
> The Chariot
> Death
> Temperance
> The Sun
> Judgement

It is the purpose of an integration class to remind you of the most important issues of the symbols we covered in the previous three classes and how those issues are embodied in specific cards. The reminder is useful because not many people can remember, much less use, the masses of information and experience we cover just by reading about them.

What we're going to do now is to reduce that mass to a few important points you can retrieve from memory whenever you need or want them. After we've done that, we'll practice a bit to see how well we've succeeded.

First, let's recap the vital issues of horses, suns, and banners. Then we'll go back and take a practical look at what we need to remember in the cards when these symbols appear.

Horses

Horses in tarot are always carrying a rider, and the two are a unit. Sometimes the rider tells the horse where to go, and sometimes the rider surrenders to his horse's knowledge and instincts. In the world of death and in psychological and spiritual landscapes, the horse knows what to do and guides the rider to his destination.

In the world of ordinary events, including all worldly considerations, the rider knows where to go and how to get there. In these cases the horse goes where he's told.

In either event, the appearance of a horse and rider tells you that an important drama or chapter in the life of a querent is in the process of working itself out.

Another important thing to remember in the relationship between horse and rider is that the rider gets his virtues from his horse. Purity, nobility, energy, heroism, radiance, certainty, sacredness—all are expressed first through the nature of the horse.

Suns

The main lesson of the sun wherever it is found is life, potential, and power. The sun is the power inside all the forms of nature—the power to be and the power to act. The sun exists both outside of everything, in the world, and inside of everything, in consciousness. It is the source of physical and psychological existence, and it is the power in everything of enthusiasm, optimism, and the will to continue. The sun acts in this way on and in everything from a rock to a human being.

The sun is also a symbol of half of all there is, the ruler of the day and all that can be associated with the day. Its appearance reminds us of the night and its darkness that is the other half of the world, which must surely follow the day in its proper time.

Sun and moon, day and night, light and dark, projecting and yielding, constantly turn around each other and become each other in an endless circle. This is what is described by the Chinese yin-yang symbol, and it is the first lesson of the lemniscate, the symbol for eternity that is the western cousin of yin and yang.

Banners

The primary purpose of banners is to project identity. A banner describes who and what someone is in a way that everyone can see and no one can miss or ignore. Banners focus awareness, rally scattered energy, demand attention, inspire, empower, and lead.

A banner proclaims, "Here I am!" It says, "Join me! Follow me! Protect me! Honor me!"

To raise a banner is to do and say all of these things.

• • •

These are the most general meanings and issues of horses, suns, and banners in tarot. But their particular applications lie in the cards where they appear. The best way to review this information and make it stick is through practical application. So we're going to do that with a reading using just these cards.

SYMBOL SPREAD:
THE RIDER'S JOURNEY

This spread is based upon the symbols studied in our classes on horses, suns, and banners. It is a very unusual spread as it makes use of only one card, which is looked at from the perspective of three

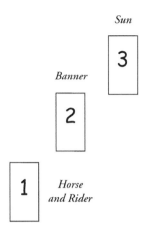

different positions. This is another subtle but powerful reading that benefits from contemplation.

The Rider's Journey is primarily a personal spread, best used as a reading you do for yourself. Its purpose is to suggest a new way to deal with an area of difficulty in your life that could benefit from a fresh approach.

It is possible to use this spread with a querent by acting as a facilitator rather than a traditional reader. This is not to say that you can't get information from the spread to tell a querent, but the insights will be much deeper if they come from the querent's own experience and perceptions.

The pictorial symbolic concept of this spread is a horse and rider (seen as a unit); the rider carries a banner and waves it in a sunlit sky.

The Process

Another thing that makes this spread different from others is the way the card is drawn. You have two choices:

1. Look through the deck until a card catches your attention and holds it.

2. Without looking at your deck, use the first card that comes to mind.

Either way is fine. You want the draw to be a conscious choice as opposed to picking it at random. It doesn't matter why the card catches your attention or comes to mind—you don't have to know that in advance.

Once you have chosen your card, place the physical card on the table face up in front of you in position #1. After you have contemplated/interpreted it from the perspective of the Horse and Rider, move it into position #2 and interpret the same card as a banner. Even though the card hasn't changed, the nature of its message will. Lastly, move the card into position #3 and reinterpret it from the perspective of the sun.

The Horse and Rider

Your card in the position of the Horse and Rider describes the energetic landscape through which you are traveling and the resources you have to work with. The horse and rider is a symbol of a drama that is going on in your life at this time. It's a developing storyline—what's happening now and in the immediate future.

The horse offers you a way to go—perhaps other than the way you're going now. If your card were a real horse, what kind of horse would it be? At what pace does it prefer to travel? As the rider, do you wish to be in control, or are you content to go where your horse leads you?

The card is a resource. It allows you to change the energy you're working with now to an energy you would prefer to work with. If you're in an intractable situation and you need another approach, the insights offered by this card will give it to you. Then it's a matter of choosing whether to use this insight or not.

The Banner

When the card becomes your banner, it becomes a symbol of your ideal identity—you can officially proclaim yourself to be this thing right now if you wish to.

The banner is a symbolic organizing principle. You can use the idea expressed on your banner to rally your energies, focus your efforts, inspire you, and eventually lead yourself to a space you want to be in.

By raising your banner, you give yourself permission to embody whatever it signifies.

The Sun

In the position of the Sun, your card describes the appropriate energy to help you along your journey. It gives you the strength and power you need to move forward and keep going.

Here, your card shows you a way you can be completely responsive to the moment. It describes what can give you pleasure and joy in the doing.

• • •

The spread doesn't require that you go in a certain direction or even predict that you will. What it does is give you the option. Because the spread uses only one card, you can display the card or bring it to mind any time you would like to invoke or recall the energy of the spread.

Any time you feel stuck, may the Rider's Journey help you along your way!

5

ARMOR, BLINDFOLDS, FEATHERS

ARMOR

Hello, and welcome to our class on the symbolism of armor in tarot. Armor appears in eight cards—The Emperor, The Chariot, Death, the four Knights, and the King of Pentacles. As usual with the imagery we discuss, there is a general symbolic meaning and a good deal of history to the image of armor and also specific applications in individual cards.

It seems as though any part of the imagery of tarot we talk about has a very long history and is fraught with meaning. In the past, we've looked at crowns and pillars and paths and crosses and suns, moons and stars. We've talked about roses and lilies and mountains and horses and banners and pools. Each one of these by itself is a symbolic gem. Together, they make a treasure so rich that it's hard to take it all in.

The symbol of armor will be another piece of treasure. For our purposes, there are three things to know about armor:

1. Where there's armor, there are weapons and war.

2. Armor can be both practical and ornamental.

3. Armor has been around as long as war and is still here today. From the looks of both current research and science fiction, it will be around for an indefinite tomorrow.

Armor was the fighting man's answer to how badly he could get hurt by lethal weapons. To survive a serious battle, he needed some serious protection. To survive several battles, that protection had to be very serious indeed. For both warrior and soldier, good armor was (and still is) the difference between minor and crippling injury, between life and death.

Armor more than weapons is the seal of the soldier or warrior. Any traveler, hunter, or crook can carry and use weapons, but armor is a long-term investment for someone whose job it is to periodically fight to the death on a field of battle.

Armor has always been expensive. Even a piece or two was once more than a poor man could afford. A good helmet or shield, the most basic forms of armor, required high craft and expensive materials to make. Plate armor and coats of mail were works of art, and a full set of armor, consisting of dozens to hundreds of parts tailormade for each user, was a major piece of engineering. And that was just for the man. If he also had a horse to protect, it could get really expensive.

But that was just the beginning. If a fighting man was successful, in the long run he became a hero or an aristocrat or both. He had to show off every so often in full military rig. That meant ceremonial armor, with special finishes, etched designs, and precious metals. It was a sign of wealth, status, and power.

This was true everywhere from China to South America, from Arabia to Japan, from the Asian steppes to the capitals of Europe. And it has been true in all times but the present, when ornamental armor has disappeared and functional armor belongs to government. But in all times and places, armor was the symbol of the fighting man who put himself in harm's way over and over again.

Whatever you may think of war and violence in general, it seems to exist everywhere and always, suggesting that organized mayhem is an archetypal aspect of humanity. Amid the brutality, cruelty, ugliness, and other nasty qualities and consequences of war, armored warriors and soldiers have developed a number of major virtues and magnificent skills and even a spirituality all their own.

Armor, more than weaponry, is a symbol of what is excellent and noble about a warrior or soldier. This is as true of the modern marine or policeman in his bulletproof vest as it was of the Roman legionary, Japanese samurai, or European knight of the past in his chain mail or breastplate.

Armor was and is the second skin of the warrior, which he puts on to face a life-and-death struggle. It is the symbol of his public acceptance of this ultimate struggle.

Which brings us to one final modern version of armor, a symbol from the realm of psychology instead of war. In this version, armor is the name given to a personal and private, unconscious, self-protective reflex that guards against mostly imaginary dangers. It's something like wearing a bulletproof vest day and night for fear of muggers. This armor is constructed and worn unconsciously and internally, out of fear and a sense of perpetual vulnerability.

Either way, armor is a form of defense. In its original physical form it is a symbol of consciousness and courage. In its psychological form it is the name of an internal unconscious dysfunction.

When you see an armored figure in tarot, you would be right in asking whether it is a sign of strength or weakness. Which brings us to the cards themselves.

The Four Knights

The four knights can be grouped together up to a point. They are all armored because the clearest symbol of a knight, what distinguishes him above all other symbols, is his armor. It is a symbol of public duty, of rank, of the specific virtues and skills of his calling, of his spirituality, and of his bond with others of his kind.

The armor of all four knights is practical rather than ceremonial, intended to protect rather than display. Every knight wears a full set of plate armor, the latest and most evolved form to arise in Europe. In each case, the knight wears a helmet and a breast

plate, as well as shoulder, arm, leg, and foot protection. Each has a spur on his foot, a plume on his helmet, and an ornamented surcoat covering his torso. None have a shield, but the surcoat serves to identify each of them, which is one of the functions of a shield.

The Knight of Wands and the Knight of Pentacles have gloves on both hands. The Knight of Swords has one gloved hand and one bare hand, and the hands of the Knight of Cups are both bare. Gloves, or gauntlets, are protection for the hands, but they are relatively clumsy. Bare hands are more vulnerable, but they are also more agile and sensitive. The bare hand of the Knight of Swords holds his sword, an indication of skill and speed with his weapon. The bare hands of the Knight of Cups are needed by a lover and a warrior of the heart.

The visor on the helmet of the Knight of Swords is raised above his head. His face is clearest, most visible, and least protected of all the knights despite his headlong charge into battle. This is one sign that he is a pure knight, air of air, transparent and abstract.

The helmet of the Knight of Wands is the most complete and defended of all the knights. He is also a pure knight, fire of fire. He is a fiery vessel containing a fiery force in a fiery world, and his helmet protects him from his own nature.

KNIGHT of SWORDS.

KNIGHT of CUPS.

The King of Pentacles

The armored foot of the King of Pentacles is a hint of the full armor hidden from sight by his robes. It is a symbol of the public servant who guards the well-being of his kingdom despite his apparent personal opulence.

The Emperor

The astrological attribution of The Emperor is Aries, and his armor, of which all you can see are the feet, is a reference to the warrior god and a reminder that The Emperor is also a warrior.

The Chariot

Here, the armor is a reference to the shell of Cancer, the astrological attribution of The Chariot. The Chariot card as a whole refers to the deeper symbolism of the Merkaba, the chariot in Ezekiel's prophetic vision that carries the knowable form of God. For this reason the armor is ceremonial rather than practical.

The breastplate is in the shape of Pisces; the black, pleated skirt refers to the deep waters of Scorpio; and the moon-shaped shoulder guards are a reference to The High Priestess, source of all the waters.

The bright square at the center of the breast plate is a symbol of the four Qabalistic worlds into which The Chariot brings all good things from above to below and from which it brings reciprocal blessings from below to above. This is a reference to the esoteric title of the card, The House of Influence.

Death

The armor of Death, though full, is purely ceremonial, since he clearly needs no protection. It is the symbol of one whose only reason for being is to serve, since it covers a reality of bare bone, unfleshed existence with no personal agenda. Death is the ultimate public servant and in this image armor is the symbol of perfect service.

From another perspective, however, his black armor is also a symbol of the self-protective hard shell of a scorpion, a reference to the card's astrological attribution of Scorpio.

The time has come to try a little exercise. It is a contemplation.

Close your eyes, breathe, and relax.

Surround yourself with darkness and rest.

Let your thoughts, desires, feelings, and sensations melt away into that darkness.

Become empty but completely aware.

Now look within. Rediscover the shape of yourself with all of its facets and complexity, shining like a gem in the night.

Re-enter the completeness of yourself as a witness.

Ask yourself this question:

Do I wear armor in any way, either as a heroic public servant or as a defended individual?

Take the time to let an answer emerge from the darkness.

Now, once again, let your personal shape dissolve in the darkness that surrounds you and rest.

The time has come to return. Take two deep breaths and, when you're ready, open your eyes but stay in a meditative state.

Take a few minutes to write down your answer to your contemplation.

*Contemplation
of the Symbol
of Armor*

BLINDFOLDS

Hello, and welcome to our class on blindfolds in tarot. Blindfolds appear in just two cards—the 2 of Swords and the 8 of Swords. But each embodies a principle of great importance and considerable subtlety, so we'll have a lot to talk about.

A blindfold creates temporary blindness and symbolizes blindness and darkness in general. It may serve one of two main purposes:

1. to prevent normal functioning in a world that requires sight;

2. to prevent distraction by the sights of the ordinary world.

In tarot the two cards with a blindfolded figure each reflect one of these two purposes.

In the world at large—in literature, mythology, and reality—blindfolds have the same implications.

• Justice and Fortune are goddesses who are blindfolded to avoid favoritism by avoiding visible distinctions.

• Hostages are blindfolded to cause disorientation and ignorance of their captors and surroundings.

• Children blindfold each other to play games like Pin the Tail on the Donkey, forcing them to use senses other than sight to make something normally simple into something difficult, unpredictable, and funny.

• In the game of Blind Man's Bluff, adults do the same thing to produce humorous erotic moments with strangers, free of the improprieties and embarrassments of foreknowledge.

• Those about to be executed are blindfolded to spare them the frightening knowledge of the moment of their death.

• Those for whom the presence of light makes it difficult to sleep blindfold themselves to produce a comforting darkness.

A blindfold can produce concentration and disorientation, knowledge and ignorance, fear and the absence of fear, freedom and constraint, darkness and light. Perhaps it can be said that a blindfold enhances a sought after or already existing physical, mental, emotional, or spiritual state.

A blindfold creates an immediate functional blindness, and in doing so it can produce either an inner light or an inner darkness. A blindfold can be more subtle than a cloth tied physically over the eyes. It can be a word or an idea, a feeling or a predilection, a deed or a memory, a talent or a samskara.

In the case of a nonphysical blindfold, its effect is to focus or filter, to redirect immediate contact with the world as it is happening through a pre-existing perspective, to darken or lighten reality, to add qualities to it or remove qualities from it, to give meaning to plain facts, or to make reality into a symbol and to transform it.

This transformation can be experienced as taking place inwardly or externally; it can be felt as positive or negative. It can be a transformation to be sought after or undone. The blindfold in the 2 of Swords is the first kind—taking place inwardly, felt as positive, and sought after. In the 8 of Swords it is the second kind—taking place externally, felt as negative, as being undone. But we'll talk more about that later.

Blindfold Exercise

For a moment, close your eyes and cover them with your hand. Imagine that you have just been blindfolded by a force outside yourself. You can't just remove your hand and open your eyes. The blindfold remains in place until whoever placed it there removes it. The darkness, though temporary, is not of your choosing. It is enforced. Be completely aware that the hand that blindfolds you, although it is your own, cannot be removed until the exercise is over.

Sit for a few moments with this awareness. Do not remove your hand from your eyes for several minutes. Then keep your hand over your eyes just a little while longer. Finally, when you are ready, take a deep breath and open your eyes.

Take a deep breath and, when you are ready, remove the blindfold and see.

Take a minute to write down the thoughts and feelings you had while you were blindfolded.

CHARACTERIZATION QUESTIONNAIRE

Here's a little questionnaire we'd like you to take. Write down each pair of words in the following list. Decide whether you associate that word with darkness or light. Then, next to the word, write D for darkness or L for light. There are a total of twenty-six words that make eighteen pairs.

Aware _____

Unconscious _____

Suffering _____

Content _____

Solid _____

Insubstantial _____

Active _____

Still _____

Masculine _____

Feminine _____

Mind _____

Heart _____

Special _____

Ordinary _____

Emerging _____

Returning _____

Body _____

Spirit _____

Obvious _____

Mysterious _____

Freedom _____

Surrender _____

Familiar _____

Unknown _____

Visible _____

Hidden _____

We chose these words to play with because they are significant to us. You can make your own list and work with it in the same way.

We characterized all the words in the list as either light or dark. This characterization makes each word richer and more personal.

But light can be experienced as positive or negative, inward or outward, obvious or mysterious, solid or insubstantial, or any of the other pairs, according to context and the temperament of the beholder. The same can be said of darkness. And what is described one way today can be turned around tomorrow.

Let's go back to our word list and take the time to make it even richer. Look at each word again and decide whether the light or darkness you associated with it earlier is inward or outward light or darkness. If it is inward, write an I after it. If it is outward, write an O.

Then decide whether that word has a positive or a negative feel to it, and write a plus or minus sign next to the previous letter. For example, for Wald, the word "suffering" is dark, outward, and negative. But the word "masculine" is dark, inward, and positive.

As you can see, each of the words in the list before you has begun to take on the richness of your own inner experience. In this way, you can increase the richness of a word many times over. In this way, a word becomes a blindfold. Do you see it?

In the same way, memories, feelings, and all the other things we have mentioned also become blindfolds. A blindfold transforms the general into the personal, the objective into the subjective.

• • •

The time has come to take a look at the cards themselves. Each of the two has a bias and intent in one direction rather than the other.

2 of Swords

The 2 of Swords looks inward into mind and spirit, toward the mysterious, invisible, and insubstantial. The blindfold serves to prevent distraction. The esoteric title of the 2 of Swords is The Lord of Peace Restored, and the 2 of any suit is the wisdom of that suit. In this case the blindfold is not temporary. It is the permanent symbol of peace and wisdom.

8 of Swords

Intuitively, the figure in the 8 of Swords appears to be experiencing the darkness of ignorance, the constraints of the outward and obvious, the limits of the physical and immediate. But the blindfold on the figure in the 8 of Swords is a symbol of optimism, of the darkness that precedes the light of initiation. The person in this card submits to being bound and hoodwinked and led to the threshold of a higher and better state.

The esoteric title of the 8 of Swords is The Lord of Shortened Force, and the 8 of any suit is the genius of that suit. In this case, the blindfolding is a temporary but repeated condition, since the process of initiation is understood to be continuous. The light of understanding on one level is the darkness that precedes initiation onto a higher level. For anyone traveling the path of personal transformation, the blindfold is a steady, and steadily changing, part of life.

• • •

In the practice of divination, you will do your best work if you have an idea of your querent's inner state. Where is your querent, including yourself when you are reading for yourself, on the circular journey of birth and rebirth, of emergence and return?

If you know that, you will know whether the blindfold is a symbol of an ordinary or a special darkness, whether it is a symbol of confusion and constraint or a tool of liberation, whether the querent is on a path or just bumbling around.

The image of the blindfold then becomes a test of your own ability to see.

FEATHERS

Hello, and welcome to our class on the symbol of feathers in tarot. Normally, we would tell you at the beginning of the class how many cards in the deck contain feathers and which ones they are. But in this case it's not so easy to do. There are a number of cards where you can't quite tell if you're looking at feathers or not. And there are several cards that contain images that are not officially feathers but look remarkably like them.

So the first thing we'd like you to do is look through your deck very carefully and separate out the cards that you think contain feathers. Then we'll make a list and arrive at a consensus of which cards we will use in this class.

Here's the list that we've compiled and that we'll work with:

Three Knights
Knight of Wands
Knight of Swords
Knight of Cups

Three Angels
Raphael in The Lovers
Michael in Temperance
Gabriel in Judgement

Others
The Fool
The Chariot
The Wheel of Fortune
Death
The Sun
Page of Wands

That is twelve cards in all that officially and obviously contain the image of the feather. We'll discuss these cards in groups or categories as well as individually. That will yield a lot of information and give you plenty to think about and work with.

Let's talk a little about feathers in general.

First, of course, feathers have practical uses. As fans, they have kept us cool. As down—in coats and vests, comforters and pillows—they have kept us warm. On arrows, to which they lend the essential quality of true and steady flight, they have been crucial to hunting and war. As quill pens, they have helped preserve in ink a thousand years of the knowledge and history of Western civilization. And as ornaments, they are perhaps the earliest and most enduring of all human adornments.

The things to remember here are coolness, warmth, softness, lightness, hollowness, flight, and beauty.

The second major function of feathers is in or as ritual objects. In ritual, a feather is the bearer of the magickal qualities of birds in general and of the particular bird it came from. The magickal lore and symbolism of birds is a subject all by itself and needs its own lesson, so all we can do here is mention it. Suffice it to say that the feathers of such birds as the eagle, the crow, the peacock, the parrot, and the pheasant evoke in almost everyone an instinctive sense of power and mystery.

Birds, and therefore feathers, are the prime symbols of flight, which gives access to the higher realms, from the upper world of the shaman to the heaven of Western religions.

In tribal ritual the world over, feathers are given as special gifts of friendship, worn as crowns and symbols of distinction, used to direct the sacred smoke of smudge and incense, and used to conduct the symphony of spirits that are said to hover over and empower acts of magick.

The third function of feathers is to enhance the magickal power of birds and transfer it to mythical and mystical beings. The feathered serpent Quetzalcoatl, supreme deity of the Aztecs; Pegasus, the mythical flying horse of Greek mythology; the feather of the Egyptian goddess Maat against the weight of which the innocence or guilt of human souls were weighed; the feathered wings of angels who rise and descend between heaven and earth— all these borrow the feather from tribal ritual to serve as a symbol of civilized divinity.

The thing to remember here is the connection of the feather to divinity, to beings of higher realms that can only be reached by flight.

Finally, we get to tarot. All the things we've spoken of so far can be useful to divination since they may arise in a reading in a purely intuitive context, although they are not specifically tarot related.

You'll get a chance to practice this later on, so remember what you've heard so far.

In tarot, feathers relate mainly to two things—to the elements of fire and air.

They relate to air because air is the only medium of flight. They relate to fire, because the highest reaches of air touch the lower border of the world of fire, the element closest to divinity or to the highest parts of yourself. It is on feathered wings that the human spirit rises to the divine fire.

Now let's look at the cards themselves.

Judgement, Temperance, and The Lovers

In all three cards, an archangel spreads his wings close to the source of a fire, giving them a fiery color. They are redder at the top and more purple or violet lower down, showing the intensity of the heat cooling as the feathers get further from the fire.

JUDGEMENT

The wings of the angel in Judgement are a Qabalistic reference. The path of Judgement on the Tree of Life is the path of elemental fire. It is the path of the awakening spirit as it begins its journey of self-knowledge. As that spirit rises, the fire on the path gets hotter and hotter, and the wings of the Archangel Gabriel get redder. The upward journey of the spirit gets more and more intense as it continues.

TEMPERANCE

Here too the reference is Qabalistic. Temperance is the direct path to the sun of Tiphereth (Beauty) at the center of the Tree of Life. The Archangel Michael spreads his wings around the corona of the sun, symbolized by the rays around the sun disk in the center of his forehead. The wings act as a protection from the light and heat of the sun and allow these energies to safely penetrate and transform any person who has come this far.

THE LOVERS

In The Lovers, the wings of the Archangel Raphael protect the human form from the intolerable blaze of divine energy. They allow a person to stand naked before the eye of God. The path of The Lovers on the Tree of Life is even higher than the spirituality of Tiphereth. It is one of five paths by which you can reach what is perfect in yourself.

• • •

In all of these cards, the feathers of the angels' wings are symbols of transcendence, as well as a form of protection that makes it possible to survive the heat of the journey of return.

The Chariot, Wheel of Fortune, and the Knight of Cups

In these three cards, the feathered wings are symbols of air, purity, and elevation. They let the spirit and the heart soar.

THE CHARIOT

The winged solar disc of The Chariot is a symbol of the Egyptian sun god rising on the hawk wings of Horus at the beginning of each new day. It is the sign of a lofty intellect and the soul's ability to hover over the Abyss, across which the path of The Chariot passes from above to below and back.

THE WHEEL OF FORTUNE

The feathers, in conjunction with the books of the creatures at the corners of the card, are symbols of Christian spirituality in the form of a reference to the four gospels.

KNIGHT OF CUPS

Court-card ranks are attributed to the elements, but each rank has a double attribution. Knights are associated with both fire and air—fire on the journey of emergence and air on the journey of return. In the Knight of Cups, the feathered wings associate this knight with the element of air.

Also, because the Knight of Cups is often interpreted as a lover, the wings at head and heel are references to Mercury, whose libido was notorious, and to his winged child, Cupid.

Knight of Wands and Knight of Swords

In these two cards, the red feathers are plumes of fire, and they remind us that the rank of knight is associated with the element of fire on the journey of emergence.

KNIGHT OF WANDS

The Knight of Wands, as pictured in the card, is a fiery knight in the suit of fire, which makes his elemental counterchange fire of fire. This is borne out by all of the other exclusively fire symbols in the card such as the salamanders and the desert landscape.

KNIGHT OF SWORDS

The image of the Knight of Swords is a combination of his fiery rank and the elemental air of the suit of swords. In the Rider-Waite-Smith deck, his elemental counterchange is fire of air. The former is indicated by the fiery plume on his helmet, the fiery shape of the cloak flying from his back, and the fiery shape of the horse's mane. The symbols of air in the card are the birds in the sky and the wind-blown trees and clouds.

Page of Wands

The rank of page, like all the court-card ranks, has a double elemental attribution. The page on the journey of emergence is associated with water and on the journey of return with earth. The fiery feather rising from the metal cap of the Page of Wands is a reference to her elemental counterchange, earth of fire.

• • •

The thing to remember about the feathers in these court cards is the intensity of their elemental symbolism.

The Fool, The Sun, and Death

In The Fool and The Sun, the red feathers are plumes of fire, connecting the crown of the head with the sun above and acting as a conduit for divine fire moving from above to below. In Death, the fiery plume is wilted, separated from the sun that lights the land of the living. Instead, the sun's fire is transmitted downward with reduced intensity, into the land of the dead. Pale and weak as it is, the sun finds its way back through Death's domain and rises again each day, completely reborn in all its original glory.

We'd like to give you a chance to put some of this information to use by doing a technique called the Voice in the Card.

First, take the twelve cards we've been discussing and shuffle them face down.

Next, draw four cards from this group and place them in front of you face up.

Now, look at just the feathers in each card. Let your gaze move from one card to the next, until the feathers of one card in particular hold your attention. Turn the other three cards face down and focus on this one card.

Completely ignore what the card means as a whole and narrow your focus to just the feather. Ignore everything else. This may be hard to do, but make an effort. The feather alone has a message for you. That message can be on any level—practical, psychological, or spiritual. Listen quietly for the message in the feather. Don't rush.

Let it come to you from within.

When you have heard the message, write it down.

Intuitive Reading Exercise

INTEGRATION:
ARMOR, BLINDFOLDS, AND FEATHERS

Hello, and welcome to our integration class for armor, blindfolds, and feathers. Do you have the notes for all those earlier classes handy? We hope so, because you'll be able to use them in this class. You'll see how in a few minutes.

We'll tell you a secret at this point, about how and why the three images of each series are chosen. Think of the series of the past—crowns, pillars, roses and lilies; paths, mountains, and crosses; moons, stars, and pools; horses, banners, and suns. This time it was armor, blindfolds, and feathers.

In each series, the integration class revealed a common denominator, a binding factor, a deep link that joined symbols with nothing obvious in common. This joining is a little piece of magic. If the connection seems logical in hindsight, that is only because the magic was successful.

The secret we're going to tell you is that, in every case, we have no idea at the beginning how it's going to turn out in the end. A group of three images present themselves to us when we need them and, essentially, ask us to have faith that all will be well.

We only discover how that happens a little bit before you do. The final piece of magic happens when we sit down to create the integration class for the series. This series has been no different than the ones before it.

But this time, we're going to engage you in the process. In the interest of true integration, we're going to issue you a two-part challenge.

First, look through your deck and take out all the cards we have studied in the three classes that make this series—armor, blindfolds, and feathers. We won't tell you what they are.

If you have your notes from those classes handy, there's nothing to it. If not, search your deck and your memory and do the best you can. Make your best effort.

Now that you have done what you can do, let us give you the "official" list:

The Fool
The four Knights
The Emperor
Page of Wands
The Lovers
King of Pentacles
The Chariot
2 of Swords
The Wheel of Fortune
8 of Swords
Death
Temperance
The Sun
Judgement

There are, as you know, other cards we might have included, but these are the ones we chose to work with. Some of the cards—Death and three of the Knights—are used twice.

The second part of the challenge is to look back over the ideas, concepts, and information of our classes on armor, blindfolds, and feathers. Once again, search your memory and your notes if you have them. Dig deep beneath the surface and find your own way to connect these three dissimilar images with a single magical bond of meaning.

You'll need some time to do this, so take it now. Do you need a hint on how to accomplish this task? If so, do the following, but only after you have read all the instructions.

Contemplation and Reading

First, close your eyes, breathe, and relax.

Surround yourself with darkness.

Clear your mind of thoughts and images and rest.

Now, allow the word "armor" to enter your thoughts and, with it, the pictures of armor in the cards as they arise in your mind's eye. Don't force it. Let it simply happen.

As you visualize the images of armor in the cards, allow yourself to remember the main ideas about armor as a symbol. Let this happen without effort. If nothing comes to mind right away, just keep at it. In time, the issues of armor will come to you of themselves.

Whenever this happens, open your eyes but stay in a relaxed and meditative state. Write down what you have come to understand about the symbol of armor.

Then, close your eyes again, and repeat the process with the symbol of the blindfold.

Finally, repeat the entire process with the image of the feather.

When you have done all this, which may take only a few minutes or perhaps a little longer, repeat the contemplative process one more time. Allow the main principles of armor, blindfolds, and feathers to swirl together in your mind until they begin to reveal what connects them. Once again, write down what you have seen.

Do all this as well as you can, but don't worry at all about the results. Just do it. Do it now.

The number of ways to see the connection between these symbols is surely more than one, and each way will have its own nuances. Let us share with you our own results from the very process you just attempted.

The main issues of armor are two:

First, it is a practical and necessary response to the danger of lethal battle, especially if it is necessary to face that danger regularly and frequently. Though the danger may be physical, psychological, or spiritual, and each requires its own kind of armor, the essence remains the same. In this case, armor is a symbol of personal and private courage and a readiness to accept an endless challenge.

The second issue of armor is ceremonial rather than practical. It is a sign of status, of the wealth and power that comes from a successful career as a warrior. It is the sign of many battles fought and survived and many more to come. In this case, armor is the symbol of a public duty and an earned honor.

All together, the issues are lethal danger, private courage, and earned honor.

Blindfolds are another matter altogether. Here, the two issues revolve around true sight and are represented by two cards. In one, the blindfold is a symbol of the inner vision that alone can see the truth. In the other, it is a symbol of the outer darkness that must be shed if the vision of the truth is to be accomplished.

A blindfold may be any experience, epiphany, understanding, or path that shuts out the clamor of external reality and allows wisdom to arise from within. A blindfold may also be any powerful deed, feeling, or thought, any memory or present reality, that focuses attention on itself to the exclusion of a deeper wisdom. Such a blindfold may or may not be a prelude to initiation.

The issues here are the light of inner truth and the darkness of distracting reality, the state of steady wisdom and the continuing trials and challenges of initiation.

Fire and air are the two issues of the symbol of the feather. Air can rise and fall at will with delicacy, grace, and perfect control. Fire rises of itself always and implacably upward, though it accepts the discipline of moving downward when it must. Both elements are most at home and at their most perfect when they are at their highest. But both can function and do their duty below.

The image of the feather is the symbol of flight. It is the buoyant, upward yearning of air and the final purifying consummation of fire. As both air and fire, the feather is a symbol of the power to move at will between above and below. It is a major symbol of emergence and return.

The reality of armor is heavy and thick, but it is the symbol of courage, virtue, and spirit.

Blindfolds are a form of real darkness that symbolize the struggle for and experience of inner light.

Feathers in reality are utterly delicate and frail. But theirs is the formidable task of carrying the light and pure down to an imperfect world and the heavy and impure upward to a state of perfection.

All three images are symbols of great and necessary good distilled from humble and unlikely forms.

This is a great lesson—one to be remembered, and one that will come in handy in the rough and tumble arena of a tarot reading.

This brings us to the final stage of an integration class, which is to use what we have learned in a reading.

First, shuffle the universe of cards we have been working with in this class.

Next, ask a question that needs answering. Write it down. Clarify and refine your question so that, as much as possible, it asks exactly what you want to know.

Finally, create a spread of your choice from the cards you just shuffled. Answer your own question, using everything you know about the cards in your spread, including the symbolism we have just discussed.

SYMBOL SPREAD:
ARMOR, BLINDFOLD, AND FEATHER

This spread is based upon the symbols studied in our classes on armor, blindfolds, and feathers. It is different from the other spreads we have worked with so far because there are several ways to approach each of the positions.

As you have learned, there are many layers of interpretation to these, and in fact most, symbols. This spread gives you the flexibility to experiment with these different ways of looking at each of the symbols, as each position can be looked at from one of several perspectives.

The layout is a simple three-card spread, consisting of the Armor (position #1), the Blindfold (position #2), and the Feather (position #3). Each card will have one of three potential symbolic meanings.

Armor
1. What protects you
2. What strengthens you
3. What weighs on you

Blindfold
1. What you're not seeing
2. What is blocking you from seeing the truth
3. How best to access your inner vision

Feather
1. How to transcend your current circumstances
2. Where to find your connection to the divine
3. What you can do to lighten up

Begin by placing the cards face down like this:

Feather

Blindfold

Armor

Before you turn over the cards, talk with your querent a little to get a sense of their question. Is it an emergent, practical issue, or does the question deal with more spiritual concerns?

Next, turn over the cards one at a time and look at the previous options for each of the symbol positions. Choose the one that makes the most sense within the context of the question. (For longer readings, you can interpret each card from more than one perspective.)

Other ways to choose:

• Let the card suggest which is most appropriate to your question.

• Let your querent choose which is most important to them.

These are our suggestions. As you review your class notes, you may find other ways of interpreting these symbols you can to add to the list. The more you understand the symbols, the richer your readings will become.

6

CASTLES, CLOUDS, GARDENS

CASTLES

Hello, and welcome to our class on the symbolism of castles in tarot. Unlike the symbols in our earlier classes, castles do not have an ancient and universal history. They are strictly European and medieval in origin. But they are powerful symbols nonetheless.

This is the next-to-last group of classes in our series on imagery and intuition in tarot. When we are done, we will have only begun to explore the symbolism of the imagery of the deck. Since there's so much left to do and no way for us to finish in a formal framework, we thought we would give you a method to do the work yourself if you wanted to.

To that end, this lesson will be different from earlier ones. It will use provocative questions and contemplation as the main engine for learning, with a little information derived from research added to round out and soften the process.

For the moment, you won't need your deck, but keep it handy.

Castle Contemplations

Here's the first question: How do you know a castle when you see one?

Think about this for a minute. Now write down your thoughts.

Most people know what a castle looks like because it's an image that belongs to our cultural heritage. But there are structures that look rather like castles but aren't. That brings us to our second question: Can you distinguish, by looking, a castle from a fortress? From a walled city? From a palace? From a tower or a strongly built house?

Think about this and write down your answer.

A castle is a recognizable structure, and recognizable structures have known functions. A house, a church, a skyscraper, a pyramid—all are built to serve a particular purpose.

The third question is: What purpose does a castle serve?

This is a difficult question because the answer is complex and many-faceted. Contemplate this question for a couple of minutes. Now write down what arose in your contemplation.

From this point on, the questions get more subtle and harder to answer.

In a previous lesson, we talked about how ordinary man-made objects often become symbols. That's because the practical uses of such objects in everyday life somehow parallel or reflect analogous functions in our inner lives.

A castle is like that. A real structure with practical functions, it is the symbol of a powerful, pre-existing inner structure. Its walls, gates, and towers; its slit windows, moat, and drawbridge; its great hall and keep; its well and storehouses; its armory and stables; its private apartments, secret staircases, and escape routes—all of these real architectural features are an outpicturing of the hidden inner home and fortress we carry within us. Your home is your castle, they say, and that is as true inside as outside.

The fourth question is: As a symbol, a living energy within, which of a castle's ordinary functions are paralleled or reflected in you? This question is fairly demanding, so take a little extra time to contemplate it. Now write down what came to you in your contemplation.

At this point, we want to lead you a little bit with more focused questions.

In the time and place where castles arose, they were, among other things, the seat of private secular power, a counterpoint to the public spiritual power of the church.

Each castle was the home of a lord and his family, fortress to his garrison of knights and soldiers, and center of order, law, peace, and safety in the midst of a lawless and violent landscape. A castle was a stronghold of privacy and personal power, a place where no outside or superior authority need be acknowledged or obeyed. The lord of a castle could do as he liked in his own domain. The quality of life within a castle depended entirely on the character of its lord, which the power of the castle distilled to its essence—benign or despotic, heroic or villainous, social or solitary.

All of this was true in its original reality. It is also true, at this moment, one way or another, inside of you as symbol.

The fifth question is: Can you find the analog or parallel of this absolute and private power in yourself?

Contemplate this question for a couple of minutes. Now, write down what you discovered in your contemplation.

As you have seen, castles served many purposes in the outside world as they also do in the world within. There is a way of dividing these purposes into the two primary energies of male and female that dominate esoteric tarot symbolism and personal psychology as well.

The sixth and final question of this lesson has two parts:

1. Which of the ordinary functions and energies of a castle are male and which are female?

2. What analogous or parallel functions and energies can you find inside yourself?

Take your time with this contemplation. When you are ready, write down what you discovered.

• • •

You've done a lot of work by this time, so you deserve a break. What comes next will be relatively easy. The time has come to pick up your deck and look through it for cards that contain castles. Now you have some criteria to judge by, so it will be interesting to see what you come up with.

We are going to work with just four cards that contain clear, unambiguous castles. They are: The Chariot, the Ace of Wands, the 2 of Wands, and the 4 of Wands.

To be clearly and unambiguously a castle and nothing else, a structure needs both walls and towers surrounding an area no bigger, and often smaller, than a small village. The 2 of Wands shows only a portion of wall, but the wall is crenelated in a way so characteristic of a castle wall that we can assume it is one if we wish.

Now let's look at these cards, first as a group and then at each in turn.

As a group, the castles in all these cards share the important characteristic of being either white or gray. White castles in fairy tale, legend, and myth are always the homes of benign forces. In the esoteric universe, castles oddly play no part that we are aware of. But white is the color attributed to Kether, the Crown, in Qabalah and to the King in alchemy. Gray is attributed to Wisdom in Qabalah and to the veil that separates pure spirit from any manifest form or substance.

Add these esoteric attributes of color to the general symbolic qualities associated with castles, and you have the overall meaning of castles in tarot. All of them are sources of high, powerful, and benign energies and gifts.

The Chariot

The castle in The Chariot is behind a wall that joins it to a city. This is a reference to the esoteric title of the card, The House of Influence, that brings all good things from above to below and from below to above. The castle is above, and the city is below.

In a reading, the castle suggests the flow of good things into the querent's life from a source above and beyond themselves.

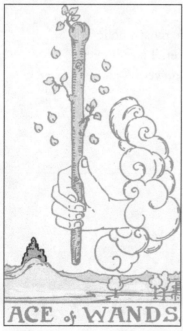

Ace of Wands

The distant white castle on a hill is a symbol of virility and the procreative power.

In a reading, this castle suggests that it is deeds that get results. It is a symbol of the potency of intent.

2 of Wands

The gray wall is part of a gray castle, seen from within rather than from outside and at a distance. It symbolizes the wisdom of the element of fire, the appropriateness of action.

In a reading, this castle is the wisdom of taking the first step, of making a beginning.

4 of Wands

This castle, with its white walls and red turrets, is a symbol of connection with the highest and purest motives and intent.

In a reading, it suggests that what has been done so far will lead to a good and happy outcome.

• • •

A special caution is useful here. With castles, more than with the other symbols we have talked about, we feel that the general significance of the image is more important and a deeper source of intuitive information than the specific references in each card.

When a castle catches your eye in a reading, look inside yourself for its meaning and remember what a castle is about. Only then add the particulars connected with the card in which it appears.

In this class, we have tried to give you a general method for inquiring into the symbolic meaning of what you see in a tarot card. It's a three-step method.

Step one is to ask provocative questions and then turn inward to find useful perspectives and knowledge through contemplation. The fact is that you know a great deal more than you think you do, and contemplation will bring that knowledge to the surface where you can see it.

Step two is research. Acquire a good set of reference books and learn to do effective searches on the Internet. Find out what you can from the best and most reliable sources and information and add that to what you learned from contemplation.

Step three is integration. Let inner and outer knowledge blend to produce a useful, internally consistent, and structurally sound picture or shape that holds the meaning you are looking for. Then, even without the stamp of approval of any external authority, what you discover will be, and remain, valid.

If you learn to do this, we will have taught you a very fine lesson indeed.

CLOUDS

Hello, and welcome to our class on clouds in tarot. Of all the objects in the visible world, clouds are the closest to not being objects at all. Clouds are always in our lives, even when they are nowhere to be seen. They pass above us most of the time, and we are hardly aware of them except as generalities. We might say, "It's a cloudy day" or "There's not a cloud in the sky!" or "It looks like rain" when the clouds look threatening. There's rarely even a notice of individual clouds.

But questions arise when you do pay attention to them. What is a cloud? When you see one, what makes you say or think, "That's a cloud"? For example, you might well ask:

How many kinds of clouds are there?

How does a cloud come to be? What makes a cloud?

Where are clouds found?

What functions do clouds serve? What do they do?

What is there in our inner selves that is cloudlike, to transform clouds from physical objects into symbols?

Think about these questions. Contemplate them. Reflect on them slowly until the answers begin to arise from within. You will find that these answers themselves begin to form a cloud of knowledge that swirls around you and subtly changes your awareness.

Let's begin to answer these questions on paper. Actually, all of these questions can be seen as facets of a single question. They can be answered as one, although the answer isn't short, or simple, either.

When we say "clouds," we are normally referring to the white puffy things that float above our heads in the sky. These are made of water vapor that rises by means of evaporation high into the atmosphere. There it cools and condenses into tiny crystals of ice or droplets of water that are light enough to float suspended in the air. These droplets gather and adhere in communities of ever-shifting shapes that we call clouds, blown on the wind until they return to earth as snow or rain.

The highest of these is called cirrus, and they are made of ice. They float like feathers, white and wispy and very far away.

Stratus clouds are lower but still made of ice crystals. They lie in layers, thicker and closer than cirrus clouds, and have distinct shapes that make patterns in the sky. These are the clouds that make dawns and sunsets beautiful with reflected sunlight.

Cumulus clouds are towers of water vapor rising thousands of feet in the air, impressive things of massive proportions that hold the promise of rain and storm and thunder and lightning.

Nimbus clouds hang low in the sky. They are ominous gray masses of moisture, hovering as close to the ground as clouds get, holding huge amounts of water that eventually come down as rain or snow. These are the clouds that make an overcast and gloomy day even when there's no precipitation. Sometimes they reach ground level as mist or fog.

Together, these clouds are the moods of the sky. They constantly come and go, arise and disappear, and they are forever changing shape. This endless movement and ceaseless change gave rise to one of the oldest of all forms of divination, called aeromancy.

Aeromancy is the general name given to reading signs, omens, and portents from events in the sky. This includes divination by wind, thunder, lightning, and the flight of birds as well as by clouds. Cloud divination specifically is called nephomancy and involves scrying with the shapes and movements of clouds over time. Hours, often days, of close observation go into a cloud divination, and there are old records of very detailed predictions with amazing predictive accuracy and depth. Nephomancy was a favorite of both Celtic and druid seers, but it has fallen into disuse in modern times. These days, no one has either the time or the ancient knowledge needed to read the clouds.

Nevertheless, clouds remain potent symbols of change. We do not personally see them arise, nor do we personally know where they go. They appear, affect us briefly, and then disappear without a trace. There is no more perfect symbol of the transitory than a cloud.

In yogic tradition, thoughts and feelings are said to be clouds crossing, but not affecting, the clear sky of consciousness. They are to be observed, but no lasting importance need be given them since they arise and disappear constantly. There is a message here that might be useful for a tarot reader to remember when a querent's problems of the moment seem intensely important.

Clouds also serve as veils, hiding or obscuring what is in, on, or behind them. They create a natural but indeterminate limit to what we can see. Airplane pilots and sailors speak of the range of visibility—what can be seen ahead before vision is obscured by clouds. Mist and fog, which are clouds that hang at ground level, add a sense of obscurity and mystery to our vision by limiting and blurring it. Clean edges and clear boundaries are lost in clouds, creating both uncertainty and a sense of possibility.

Clouds separate what is above from what is below. Ordinary life is always lived below the clouds. What is above them is too rarified, too thin, too abstract to support the life we know. Above the clouds in the physical world, space extends away infinitely. In the inner world, it is the place of spirit, of heaven, of fairy tale and myth, of those things we speak of but rarely, if ever, experience.

A pillar of cloud was said to have guided the tribes of Israel as they wandered in the deserts of Sinai. Angels appear from out of clouds or ride on them. Those who arrive in heaven are pictured as walking on clouds. The castle of the giant in the tale of *Jack and the Beanstalk* rests on a landscape of clouds. The entire pantheon of Greek gods resides on Mount Olympus, above the clouds. When a person's head is in the clouds, their awareness is in a high and impractical place.

But clouds can also be harbingers of doom, gloom, and disaster. Storm clouds can bring flood and blizzard. The mushroom cloud of a nuclear explosion is a cloud of radioactive dust, the ultimate symbol of man-made death and destruction.

The modern theory that accounts for the end of the entire race of dinosaurs, which ruled the earth for sixteen million years, is that a cloud of dust raised by a meteor strike was so vast and encompassing that it instantaneously changed the entire climate of the earth. It created an environment in which dinosaurs could not live.

Clouds of volcanic ash and gas are symbols of one or another form of disaster. Clouds of smoke guarantee that there is fire below. Sometimes, the fire that causes the cloud of smoke is destructive, and sometimes it is not.

When a steak is sizzling on the grill, the cloud of smoke that arises from it is savory and is a promise of the meal ahead. The cloud of smoke that arises from a stick of incense or a bunch of sage can create an atmosphere of peace, tranquility, and sacred space.

Clouds can be signs and symbols of obscurity and dysfunction. We speak of clouded judgment, a mental condition in which any decision made is likely to be the wrong one. Clouded vision is the inability to see or understand truly and accurately. A cloud of gloom permeates the atmosphere of a time and place with emotional darkness. A cloud of suspicion hangs over and threatens the future of whoever is beneath it. Cloudy water is, by definition, impure, not altogether itself, bearing possibly unwanted material in suspension, and making the water perhaps dangerous and unfit to drink.

When clouds are thick and pervasive over a landscape, depression and the incidence of suicide increases. When clouds are rare, the brilliant unshielded sun creates intense and fiery landscapes and temperaments.

But mostly, clouds are known for bringing the fertile rain. They are the visible symbol of the cycle of water that gives life to us all. We literally could not live without them.

As the moods of the sky, they reflect our inner weather—stormy, whimsical, glorious, oppressive, dreamy, damp, cheerful, energetic, lazy, mysterious, frightening, promising.

But they are also symbols in tarot. There they are first, foremost, and most frequently, symbols of the element of air, the element in which they appear. For this reason, they figure prominently in the entire suit of swords, which is traditionally associated with the element of air.

Second, they are symbols of divinity and divine

THE LOVERS.

JUDGEMENT.

WHEEL of FORTUNE

THE WORLD.

ACE of WANDS

205

things, of mystery, the unseen, and the unknown. As such, clouds appear beneath the angels in The Lovers and Judgement, at the four corners of The Wheel of Fortune and The World, and as the mysterious origin of the hand that appears in all the aces and the 4 of Cups. In the 7 of Cups, they are the sign of imagination, fantasy, and potential.

Whenever clouds in tarot catch and hold your attention, take the time to remember their general and tarot-specific symbolism. Add this knowledge to your reading, and it will immediately become richer and more fertile.

GARDENS

Hello, and welcome to our class on gardens in tarot. As it turns out, this is a big subject—bigger than we had thought when we began to do the research. But the essence is still simple. In the end, after all is said and done, gardens are living metaphors for perfection.

Everywhere in the world, where there is or was civilization, there have been gardens. In Egypt, although there are only very few archaeological remains, the ancient records speak of gardens belonging to temple, palace, and home. Shade, water, perfume, and fruit surrounded the senses with pleasure and relief from a relentless sun. Caged animals and birds entertained the viewer, who would, of course, have been either rich or powerful. The poor and the ordinary had no access to these pleasures.

In China, gardens have been part of things since the beginning, which is about as far back as human history goes. The Chinese sensibility sees the universe as being on three levels—heaven above, earth below, and humanity in between. It was understood that the reason and justification for human existence was to balance and harmonize the powers of heaven and earth. The harmonious flow of yin and yang, of in and out breathing, of life and death, of blossoming and withering, was the sign of perfection. Peace was the peace within, when harmony was achieved. Nothing was greater than this. The rules, laws, and customs that ensured an harmonious existence bound emperor, mandarin, sage, soldier, and peasant. A Chinese garden was designed to reveal the principles of harmony to the eye, the heart, and the spirit.

In Japan, the Zen garden was made out of sand, gravel, and stone. The Japanese predilection for contemplation, for solving koans, made of seemingly irresolvable contradictions and impossibilities, was incarnated in beautiful, serene puzzles that taught the mind and the soul through the eye. A Zen garden was not made to be walked through but to be observed while seated in meditation or while drinking tea in a ritual that paralleled the nature of the garden on a deep level.

The Middle East had its own version of the metaphor of garden as perfection. Our modern word "paradise" comes from the Persian "pardeiza," which meant "walled or enclosed garden."

In a Persian garden, a verdant oasis arose from an arid land-scape—literally a heaven on earth. It was a formal garden, an ideal realized in a perfect aesthetic. Although Persia had several types of gardens, built to different standards, the most ideal was built around a central pool, which had four streams rising from it and flowing to four quadrants. This pattern was derived from descriptions of Eden in the Old Testament.

When the Mongols invaded Persia, they took the Persian garden with them to India and mixed with it their own grandeur and epic style to create gardens in which whole palaces were an integral part of the overall design. The most famous example of a Mogul-Persian garden is the Taj Mahal.

In Islam generally, the garden is a metaphor for paradise, a place of perfect delight and a reward for living and dying in a virtuous manner. The promise of this reward is enough by itself to motivate people to martyrdom.

Islam, in the form of the Moors, brought their gardens to Spain and Italy. Spain, in particular, adopted the Moorish style in many things, including gardens. Moorish gardens are like open living rooms, halls, and rooms containing fountains, potted trees, and flowers; they are hidden behind outer walls and inside of and between galleries, but they are open to the sky—completely private and secluded from worldly eyes but visible to the eye of God.

In Italy, the lineage of gardens comes primarily from Rome. The Roman garden, like Rome itself, was practical and hedonistic. People needed water and shade for relief from the hot Mediterranean sun, so

Roman gardens were cool retreats. They were built around grottos, caves, and mountain hollows. Shaded paths led to fountains; porticos bordered canals, and baths could be found cooled by sea breezes. Everywhere there were statuary and architectural adornments— small open buildings made of roofs supported by columns, trellises covered with vines, topiary and obelisks, vases containing trees and flowers, and benches for resting. The garden was pure enjoyment for the body and the senses, a place to rest and revive.

The Italian garden became the exact model for the formal English garden of the seventeenth and eighteenth centuries. Roman landscape architecture was copied scrupulously and gave the English landed gentry the additional pleasure of a hugely conspicuous status symbol. To the grandiose and formal, the English added the esoteric and symbolic. This came in the form of mazes and labyrinths made of box hedges, and small but elaborate and exquisite temples built to embody the principles of Freemasonry, which was a powerful influence in the political and intellectual life of the time.

But Europe had its own tradition of medieval gardens. There were herbers, which were small gardens enclosed by low walls. They had turf seats around the perimeter and beds of fragrant herbs in the center. The herber, though small, was a formal garden, fragrant and meditative, a place of deep relaxation and retreat.

Then there was the flowery mead, which was a meadow of closely mowed grass artistically covered with wildflowers. It was a place to walk, run, lie down, picnic, and play. There were also utilitarian gardens where vegetables, spices, and medicinal plants were grown. These could be found on the grounds of every monastery and hospital.

Manor gardens all over Europe included statuary, arbors, gazebos, cloistered walkways, lattices and trellises, terraced lawns, and parterres (made of colored sand, gravel, stone, or flowers, which made patterns that could be seen from above from windows or hills). An extension of the manor garden, which could be very large all by itself, was the park. The park added woodlands and meadows and was stocked with animals and birds for hunting.

Renaissance villa gardens were another form of extravagance for the rich and powerful of Europe. These gardens tended to be rambling, informal, and pretty; their winding paths, fountains and statuary, trees and flowers were chosen for scent and beauty and were interspersed with hidden benches for trysting lovers. These gardens were constructed purely for pleasure.

In modern cities, we are all familiar with botanical gardens, which remind urban dwellers that nature does exist and is pleasant.

Of all the many kinds of gardens that we have no space to describe here, there is one more, a special kind, that needs mention because it serves a purpose we should include in our theme of gardens as metaphors for the high and perfect. That is the Mary garden.

A Mary garden is a development of religious nature symbolism in which the figure of the Virgin Mary is surrounded by some of her symbolic flowers. This is a meditative garden whose entire purpose is to use flower symbolism to evoke Mary's special spirit and the religious issues that are connected with her. The fullest impact of such a garden is said to come from first cultivating and then beholding it. In this way her praises are proclaimed and meditated on. The garden tells her story in a way similar to a medieval rose window or illuminated book of hours. Among the flowers most sacred to Mary are the rose and lily, a repeated theme in tarot.

Finally, we need to speak of the quintessential garden: the Garden of Eden. In the creation story at the foundation of three religions, humanity is born in the garden. It is in this garden that a human being knows bliss, innocence, and perfection. It is from this condition that man and woman were expelled and to this condition that they hope to return. It is here, in the garden where they were born, that they are what they were meant to be. This garden is perhaps the ultimate religious, mystical, philosophic, and esoteric goal and the greatest of all symbols.

Now let's look at gardens in the cards themselves. Find the cards in your deck that have a garden in them. As usual, it isn't altogether clear which cards contain what we're looking for. But in this case, it is less important than in most. All the modern meanings in tarot derive directly from or are colored by the esoteric mindset and preoccupation of a century ago.

In that universe of Qabalistic and alchemical symbolism, there is only one garden—Eden. Every card that clearly contains, or even hints at, a garden is speaking of Eden in one way or another.

Maybe the one thing to remember about the source of meaning in tarot from the nineteenth century onward is that the entire deck and every card in it is a picture of the Tree of Life in whole or in part. The Tree of Life stood at the center of the Garden of Eden and overshadowed it. The Tree of the Knowledge of Good and Evil, whose fruit caused the Fall, is said to be only a branch of the Tree of Life, as is every other tree that bore every fruit that was good and nourishing for humanity to eat.

In tarot, every garden refers to Eden—to innocence, bliss, and perfection; to order, peace, and safety; to cultivation—of both inner virtue and outer reward. Rather than speak of the specific intent of gardens in individual cards, remember these general issues instead. Before we finish, though, here are some references for two cards that you might find useful and enjoyable.

Ace of Pentacles

The Ace of Pentacles, like all the aces in tarot, is a divine gift, the gift of a whole world and an element of creation. The element is earth, all that is solid and real; the world is the world of manifestation, the stage where the drama of life is played out.

In the Ace of Pentacles, that world and that element are presented as the gift of a garden—the garden of earthly delights. In this garden is everything that sustains us and makes us happy. The real world, the one that we know and experience on a daily basis, is not a vale of tears and suffering but a place of joy. This is an affirmation and a promise of tarot.

The Star

The Star is the landscape of Eden itself. In the original Golden Dawn symbolism, the landscape of this card contains two trees, and the urn pouring water on the ground creates four streams rather than five.

The two trees were the Tree of Life and the Tree of the Knowledge of Good and Evil. In the Rider-Waite-Smith deck, only the Tree of Knowledge remains, bearing the ibis, bird of Thoth, master of knowledge. The Tree of Life is not shown here, presumably because it is everywhere.

The four streams of the original symbolize the four rivers that flowed from the central waters of Eden—rivers of fire, water, air, and earth that together create the universe. Waite shows five streams, the symbol of the senses and the lower world of nature. It is possible that he uses the five streams as one of his occasional blinds that disguise a piece of secret esoterica.

The pool is likewise the source of all the waters, and the ripples in it are the symbol for the outward-flowing energy of all the four rivers that arise from it. All together, The Star is a picture of paradise before the Fall.

• • •

Whenever you see a garden or a reminded of a garden in a tarot card, let it be an omen for good, and you won't be wrong.

INTEGRATION: CASTLES, CLOUDS, AND GARDENS

Hello, and welcome to our integration class for castles, clouds, and gardens. There are many castles in the world, an infinite number of clouds, and more gardens than you can count, including the ones in tarot. What makes all of this meaningful, what makes it all important, is that there is one castle, one cloud, and one garden that exist inside us all. That one has a billion variations, but there's only one for all that. If you can discover the meaning of that one inside yourself, you'll know it in everybody. Then you will become a very good reader indeed.

Castle, cloud, and garden—these three images bring to mind a hundred issues that are linked together in thematic contrasts. Control, freedom, harmony; anxiety, unconcern, serenity; construction, process, growth; preparedness, spontaneity, cultivation—these are some thematic issues that occur immediately, but there are many more.

Create your own and learn from each one. Each contrast and the issues that make it are keys. They unlock secrets. You yourself are a secret castle, an unknown landscape above the clouds, a hidden garden.

For a moment, let's look at just one word, one term from one thematic contrast—the word "control"—and see what can be learned from it. It's a simple word, but as a key, it opens a door to self-inquiry.

Control, we think, is an issue for everyone. It lives in you and expresses as you. You can examine it with questions. For example: How good is your self-control? How well do you control your appetites, passions, and reflexive responses? Do you need to? Do you want to?

To what extent do you feel you are in control of your life? Do you want to be? Do you make things happen? Let things happen? Help them happen?

How do you feel about coercion, the exercise of control over others by force? If you have children or employees, or subordinates or dependents of any kind, do you approve of coercion as a means of control? Is there a limit? What is it? How do you feel when coercion is applied to control you?

We are all controlled to some extent by social coercion, sometimes subtle and sometimes bare knuckled. Law, custom, convention, propriety, morality—all exercise a control over us pretty continuously. These are all issues of the castle—the walls of control constantly constrict and shape us. If we shape up, to the extent that we do, we are deemed acceptable and worthy of inclusion, protection, and reward. If not, to the extent that we don't, we are marginalized, rejected, excluded, and sometimes punished.

How well do you fit in? How comfortable are you with the pervasive controls of society? Have you internalized these controls until they are a part of you? Do you openly rebel? Do you secretly rebel but pretend to fit in? Have you ever lived in a time or place where social controls were rigid and tyrannical? Have you ever imposed a tyranny of control on others?

We'll stop here, although we could go on. This is some of what arises from a single word that arises from a single image. The power of this process of self-inquiry is clear. It awaits you with a turn of a card, so there is power in that turning. The more you know, the more powerful the turn of a card becomes.

Three-Card Reading

In tarot, knowledge is raw power, but technique makes that power useable. The time has come to take out your deck. Look through it and pull out the first twelve cards that contain a castle, a cloud, or a garden. Put the rest of the deck aside and shuffle these twelve cards face down.

Now ask yourself a question that truly needs an answer. Write it down. Carefully revise your question so that it asks exactly what you want to know, neither more nor less.

Draw three cards from the stack of twelve and turn them up for a three-card reading. Pay careful attention to the castle, cloud, or garden in each card and read only those symbols and nothing else. Forget what the card means. Don't read reversals.

Remember the specific tarot meanings of the symbol in each card. Remember the general meanings as well. Then look inside yourself for the expression of the one castle, cloud, or garden that lives in you as you. Take your time. Do a good reading.

• • •

Now it's time for a little R & R after all the heavy stuff. Put away cards, paper, pen, everything.

*Journey
for Rest
and
Relaxation*

Close your eyes, breathe and relax, and listen.

Above you are the clouds in the sky. Become aware of them.

Beyond the clouds is a landscape, just above them. Go there now and look around.

In the distance is a castle. It belongs to you. Go there.

Enter and look for a room that contains a beautiful box. Find the box and open it.

In the box is a key, the key to your own garden of perfect delight. Pick up the key and let it take you to the entrance of your garden.

Enter your garden. Spend some time there. Observe, create, cultivate, and enjoy.

Your garden brings rest to your mind, peace to your heart, serenity to your spirit, and pleasure to your senses. No harm can come to you here, nor can any harm be done by you. Enjoy, enjoy, enjoy until it's time to return.

When you are ready to return, find the place where you entered your garden and stand before that entrance.

Hold your key and let it take you to the room in your castle that contains the box.

Put the key in the box and exit the castle into the landscape above the clouds.

Descend from the clouds and re-enter your body.

Wiggle your fingers and toes. Become conscious of the room around you.

Take two deep breaths and, when you're ready, open your eyes.

Welcome back.

SYMBOL SPREAD: CASTLE, CLOUD, AND GARDEN

This spread is based upon the symbols studied in our classes on castles, clouds, and gardens. This is a very simple, all-purpose spread that you'll find useful in addressing almost any type of question. You can use it as a stand-alone reading or as part of a longer, multi-spread session. Used in conjunction with another symbol spread (or other layout of your choice), the Castle, Cloud, and Garden spread can add a useful layer of perspective.

The layout is a three-card spread. Begin by placing the cards face down, like this:

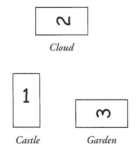

Castle

1. What is within your control.

The castle is your stronghold. It provides your resources and acts as your power base. This is where you have the fortitude to handle and/or change things, either on your own or with help.

Cloud

2. What is beyond your control.

Clouds are a force of nature that you cannot personally affect. The card that appears in this position will address something that you do not possess the ability or resources to change. You may have already discovered that attempting to do so is futile. Remember, however, you always have control over the way you choose to react and behave.

Garden

3. What can be cultivated to bring you pleasure.

A garden brings rest to the mind, peace to the heart, serenity to the spirit, and pleasure to the senses. The energy of the card in this position can be worked with to bring you one or more of these things. Even when the card appears to be uncomfortable, it contains the seed of a fruitful outcome.

7

RIVERS, TOWERS,
ANGELS, TEMPLES

RIVERS

Hello, and welcome to our class on rivers in tarot. We are coming to the end of our current work on symbolism, and this last series of four images will, we hope, complete the work in essence, even though there's a great deal more to explore in detail. In this completion, we hope a certain understanding or feeling will begin to light a darkness you might not even have noticed was there.

Rivers are delicate and complex because they are alive, and because they're alive, they can be understood both plainly and deeply. Rivers are real, and they are mythic and symbolic. The best place to start to understand them is in reality. There they have a form, a function, and a process that allows myth and symbol to arise.

We'll begin by asking a by now familiar pair of questions:

1. What is a river?

2. How do you know one when you see one?

A river is a large stream of flowing water. The general scientific term that includes all flowing water is "stream."

Every river is different, but all rivers are alike in some things. Just as, say, a human being has a head, a torso, arms, legs, and feet, all rivers have a source, a channel, tributaries, and an end. And just as each person has an identity, each river does also.

A river arises from a source—always. A river flows downward—always. Its flow is fresh water—always. It comes to an end—always. But each of these generalities has variations.

Some rivers are born from springs of fresh water that emerge from the earth. Some begin as melted ice from a glacier. Some begin their flow from a lake or swamp. Often a river starts as rain or melted snow on a mountain. All of these sources can be found at high places on the earth. And, of course, all of these sources have their own origin in the clouds.

Water begins high and seeks the lowest level it can find. From high ground there is always a path that leads downward. The quickest path downward from its source becomes the channel of a river. When it can go no lower, the flow of a river comes to an end.

According to the magickal philosophy of tarot, it is exactly in this way that manifestation of all kinds takes place. This is the way the world is said to be created and is also how we create our own lives. Take a moment to think about something in your life now that is seeking the level of manifestation.

Rivers start small, maybe no bigger than a trickle of raindrops running down a tree trunk or a hillside. These rivulets join where their courses meet in a single larger downward-moving channel.

Smaller channels meet again and again in larger ones. They form creeks and streams, which may in turn form pools and lakes, whose overflow pours their contents ever downward in small rivers that converge in ever-deeper, ever-wider channels. From these tributary sources rivers emerge—flows of water so large, so well defined, that they acquire names and identities.

In the same way, each human life begins as a flow of pure possibility and, little by little, is influenced and added to by a multiplicity of other lives. In time, a new, unformed, and delicate infant awareness becomes a full, well-defined adult stream of consciousness.

For a moment, close your eyes. Breathe and relax.

Let your memory wander back, up the stream of your personal history toward its source. As you journey back in time, remember some of the streams of life that entered and joined with yours to make you who you have become. Be aware that you are the sum of many living streams, not just yours alone.

Take two deep breaths and, when you're ready, open your eyes.

River Memory Exercise

• • •

Some rivers reach the sea. Some end in lakes, some in swamps or bogs. Some rise directly into the sky as they evaporate under the heat of a desert sun. And some disappear below the ground into the darkness of the mysterious earth. Each life, too, has its own style of ending.

From beginning to end, the essence of a river is freshness. It is fresh water, the water that directly sustains the life of all air-breathing creatures, as well as the creatures that swim in it and live beneath its surface. It is flowing fresh water that cleans with its purity and movement and feeds the surrounding earth the moisture it needs for life.

Flow of Life Experience

Once again, close your eyes. Breathe and relax.

Take a long moment to look deep inside yourself until you find the freshness of the steady flow of your life. When you have done this, experience it fully. It will make you new. If you can't find that freshness right away, find a way to invoke it. It is there inside you always. It is the essence of your life.

Take a deep breath and, when you're ready, open your eyes.

• • •

In its flow, a river picks up and carries with it the soil from its bed and banks and the organic decay of all that lives and dies in it. The silt formed from this material becomes a rich organic compound that a river often deposits at its mouth, creating a delta of super-rich soil. The entire civilization of Egypt, past and present, depended on the ever-repeating Nile floods to bring water and rich soil to its desert banks for farming. For lack of these floods over a period of years, a whole empire once built around the Nile failed and disappeared.

Rivers would always, of themselves, be pure, flowing fresh water but for the presence of civilized humanity along their banks, which pours into them its own endless stream of toxic waste. Rivers carry away the poisonous by-products of human existence, including their sins. It is at this point, at the juncture of human shortcomings and natural perfection, that both rivers and lives become mythic and symbolic.

In reality, a river is a life, a living thing in its own right, in the way that all the forms of the natural earth are alive. But in myth and symbol, rivers enter human consciousness and dwell there as stories and lessons.

The great rivers of the world each have an identity that influences the human landscape through which they flow. The Nile, the Amazon, the Mississippi, the Congo, the Danube, the Ganges only need to be mentioned to evoke the feeling-tone of the world that surrounds them. Speak the names of the Thames, the Seine, the Rio Grande, and you can see the places through which they flow and conjure their histories. Stories, myths, and legends surround real rivers and give birth to rivers that live only in our imagination.

Let me give you a couple of examples. These are just the short versions of elaborate tales, but you'll get the idea.

It is said in India that the Ganges is a holy river. In fact, it is the holiest of all rivers, and everyone in India comes to it on pilgrimages, at times of birth and death, and to wash away their sins.

The Ganges arose in the following way. An ancient king had 60,000 sons, and it became necessary for the king to send all his sons on a quest. In the course of that quest, they unnecessarily interrupted the deep meditation of a great sage. The sage, aroused from his meditation, saw that the young men were the cause of his disturbance, and he reduced all 60,000 of them to ashes with a single glance. Thereafter, the sons of the king remained as troubled spirits, unable to enter heaven, permanently weighed down by the consequences of their folly.

Another younger son of that same king prayed with all his pure heart that his brothers be cleansed of their sin and freed from their bondage. The gods heard his prayer. Brahma, the creator of the world, collected sweat from the feet of Vishnu, the maintainer of the world. From this holy moisture, Brahma created the goddess Ganga and gave her the task of descending to earth

225

to purify the ashes of the king's 60,000 sons, so that they could at last attain paradise.

Ganga was miffed at being given a task that she felt was less than appropriate for her, and she swept down in three great torrents that would have flooded the earth had not Shiva, god of destruction, caught the waters on his brow and broken their fall. Being propitiated by the king's young son, Ganga followed him to the sea and then to the underworld to fulfill her mission.

When Mother Ganga fell to earth, she came down on the summit Mount Meru, the peak that is said to be the center of the earth. She encircled the golden city of Brahma, which is located on the summit, nine times before dividing into four streams that flowed down the mountainside in the four cardinal directions. These four rivers flowing down from the top of the center of the world created the world pyramid that floats on the ocean of the cosmos.

Ganga's descent to earth in three torrents and her division into four rivers correlates with the myth of the Seven Ganges, which Hindus today identify with the seven rivers of India. Because her waters were touched by all three of India's trimurti, or trinity, of Brahma, Vishnu, and Shiva, the Ganges is said to be the essence of holiness, which purifies all she touches.

The Ganges is a river in the real world that has entered mythology and become a symbol. Now let's look at some rivers that rise directly from mythology itself.

In Greek mythology, there are five rivers that flow within or around Hades, the underworld. These are:

1. Acheron—river of woe, separating the land of the living from the land of the dead. The ferryman Charon would take newly dead souls across the river into Hades at the place guarded by Cerberus, the dragon-tailed, three-headed dog. Cerberus let souls enter but does not let them leave.

2. Cocytus—river of lamentation. To cross the river Acheron, a soul needed to pay Charon with a coin called an obol, which was placed in the mouth of the deceased before a proper cremation. Those who could not pay had to wait for 100 years on the banks of the Cocytus, which eventually flowed into Acheron.

3. Phlegethon—river of fire, which burned but never consumed fuel. In Dante's *Divine Comedy*, Phlegethon flows with boiling blood and is part of the seventh circle of hell, reserved for tyrants, murderers, and those guilty of sins of violence.

4. Lethe—river of forgetfulness. Drinking from this river caused total loss of memory. Before reincarnation, souls were made to drink the waters of Lethe so they would not remember past lives when they were reborn.

5. Styx—river of hate, another river that surrounds Hades and circles it nine times. It was in this river that Achilles was dipped by his mother when he was an infant to give him complete protection and therefore immortality. Only his heel, by which his mother held him, did not enter the water. It was through this small vulnerability that death finally came to Achilles, by way of a poisoned arrow shot through his heel.

The Styx was so respected by the gods that they swore oaths by it. If a god gave his oath on the River Styx and failed to keep his word, he was forced to drink from the river itself. The water was said to be so foul that the god would lose his voice for nine years.

In later classical times, the legends of the Styx and the Acheron were joined, and it was across the Styx that Charon was said to row his ferry.

Four of the rivers, Acheron, Cocytus, Phlegethon, and Styx, met in a great marsh at the center of Hades where they ended their flow.

These myths, legends, and stories do not find their way into tarot, but they play an important part in the spirituality of their times and places. Specific to tarot in its symbolism is the mythology of Eden, contained in the literature of Qabalah. It is a large and very rich story, with many embellishments and meanings, but here we'll give just enough to help us find the rivers in tarot, which are mostly invisible and as important as they are hidden.

It is said that a river arose in Eden from out of the roots of the Tree of Life. That river divided into four, each of which flowed from the Tree of Life into the garden in one of the four cardinal directions. Each river flowed with the energy of one of the four elements attributed to the letters of the name of God, who created the garden. So there was a river of fire, a river of water, a river of air, and a river of earth. All of these rivers can be found in tarot, but where? In the qabalistic story, these four rivers ran through and then out of Eden, to form from their energies the four worlds that together make the world that we know, and also make us what we are.

In tarot, the elemental world formed from the river of fire is the entire suit of wands. The river of water becomes the world of the suit of cups. The river of air becomes the world of the suit of swords. And the river of earth becomes the world of the suit of pentacles.

Close your eyes. Breathe and relax.

Surround yourself with darkness and rest there for a moment.

Now, in the darkness of your own original consciousness, see one of the four rivers—of fire, water, air, or earth—and feel it flowing through you. Do this until the feeling is clear and strong. Remember the feeling so you can describe it later.

It is time to return.

Become aware of your surroundings and, when you are ready, open your eyes.

Elemental
River
Meditation

• • •

These four elemental rivers have another form of expression in tarot, even less visible than the suits. Take a moment to look through your deck for The High Priestess, The Emperor, The Hierophant, The Lovers, and The Chariot.

You may well know by now that each of the Major Arcana is said to be a path on the Tree of Life, which in Qabalistic terms is the shape of each of the four worlds. In the middle of the Tree of Life is a vast space, called the Abyss. The Abyss separates divinity from both spirit and nature, above from below. This division exists in each of the four worlds and also in each of us.

The vastness of the Abyss is crossed by the five rivers of Eden: the original headwaters and the rivers of the four elements. The High Priestess has the astrological attribution of the moon. Her path begins in Kether, the Crown, the very top of the Tree of Life, and flows across the Abyss to Tiphereth, Beauty, at the spiritual center of the tree. Hers is the original river from which all others arise.

The astrological attribution of The Emperor is Aries. His is the river of fire that crosses the Abyss from Wisdom to Beauty. The Hierophant is Taurus, the river of earth that crosses the Abyss from Wisdom to Mercy. The Lovers is Gemini, the river of air that crosses the Abyss from Understanding to Beauty. And The Chariot is Cancer, the river of water that crosses the Abyss from Understanding to Severity.

These five rivers, the five paths, are all that connect above to below, in the world and in us. They hold us together and unify us. They let our natures flow freely between our highest and lowest potential. These are the hidden rivers in tarot and in us.

Now look through your deck and take out all the cards that contain visible rivers. We'll list some of the many functions of rivers and then apply them to what we see in the cards.

Rivers are and have always been:

- sources of food and water, hygiene, and power
- boundaries and borders
- obstacles and defenses
- highways and landmarks

They create beautiful, sometimes breathtaking, landscapes with their passing, like canyons, gorges, and waterfalls. They are symbols of flow; of time and timelessness; of change and changelessness; of purity, transformation, and rebirth; of life and the continuation of life. They are the home and even the embodiment of gods, goddesses, and spirits of all kinds, and they lend their identities and characters to the landscapes, real and mythic, through which they pass.

Look at the cards you have selected that have rivers in them and assign to each of them one or more of the functions we have named or others you may think of yourself.

Contemplate all the rivers in tarot and the function that each of them serves.

If you remember what you discover in your contemplation of these rivers and apply this knowledge in your readings, they and you will be deepened, and your querents will be better served than they know.

Rivers
in Tarot
Contemplation

TOWERS

Hello, and welcome to our class on towers in tarot. As our study of imagery approaches its conclusion, it feels more and more numinous. Symbols take on meaning like shapes emerging from a mist, and we see things we never knew, or only guessed, were there. Towers are going to be like that, and we hope you enjoy the process.

Some things are the way they are with no help from us. The sun hangs in the sky; rivers run downhill; pools are cool, dark, and deep; and mountains rise above the plain, all by themselves. In themselves, they are innocent of meaning.

Other things are what they are only because we made them that way. Castles, pillars, banners, and crowns perform the functions we invented them to perform and they would not exist but for us.

All these things, natural and artificial alike, are real, and they exist in what we call the real world. These same things are also symbols, and they exist, among other places, in the symbolic universe of tarot. There they serve the purpose that all symbols serve, which is to explain us to ourselves.

And we need explaining. Our natural, physical shape and our normal qualities and abilities in themselves have no meaning and explain nothing. Those things make us creatures among other creatures, nothing more. And as creatures, like other creatures, we should be content with what we are. To some extent, for a part of us, that is true.

As tarot readers, we are thoroughly familiar with this state of contentment. It comes to us in the form of querents, whose primary wish is to improve and enrich their personal experience of the natural world, not transform or explain it.

But another, equal part of us is not content. We find ourselves and the world mysterious. We ask questions and have ambitions. We experience our natural state as limited, insufficient. We deny that limitation, both inner and outer, and strive for mastery, both inner and outer.

The tower is, perhaps, of all the symbols in tarot, the prime symbol of our discontent and the quest for mastery, for power.

The natural phenomenon from which the symbol of the tower arises is its opposite, and it is a symbol in itself. That is the force of gravity, the ultimate symbol of limitation, of all that holds us down. You could say that gravity as a symbol is the power of the status quo, of things as they are. Under the influence of gravity, nature changes in detail but never in its essentials. Gravity is the power of the real. It is the natural attraction that objects have to each other. It provides the ultimate orientation by letting all living things know without question which way is down and that that way is always the way to the center. The objective universe literally stands on this orientation, which could be said to be quintessentially feminine. In tarot terminology, it is the defining quality of the elements of earth and water and the suits of pentacles and cups.

Towers are masculine, symbols of transformation. They rebel against nature, using fire (will) combined with air (intelligence) to raise the material universe upward against the pull of gravity.

Towers exude pride and a sense of power, the ambition and ability to rise above the natural state. Since they cannot be built by individuals acting alone, and since they demand enormous resources of wealth, skill, and time to build, they imply that the human impulse to verticality is not isolated but suffuses the human community.

Of course, verticality occurs in nature, but in spite of that, the natural state tends to be flat, low, rooted, or floating or falling. All creatures on the earth, including human beings, fish, and birds, live in primary reference to the surface of the earth.

Fish can and do go up and down in water as birds do in air. Both are buoyed by their medium and rise or sink in it at will, as land creatures can and do climb trees and mountains. But they all remain within their natural limits and boundaries.

Only human beings can and do ignore and resist the natural limits of gravity. And the first successful attempt to rise above the surface of the earth is the building of towers. A tower is a proclamation of human resistance to limit.

Natural manifestation of all kinds is always represented and understood as a spiritual or magical flow downward from high to low. The building of a tower reverses this process, moving from low to high. It reverses the energy of flow.

When a tower is built, the builders seek their own elevation. They depend on no one and nothing but themselves, generating and manifesting power entirely from within. They are both giver and receiver. Even in the case of sacred building, as in church towers and steeples, or pagodas or minarets or ancient ziggurats, the physical elevation of these structures includes an implied statement of the triumphal power of the builders. This is the essence of the story of the Tower of Babel, where the pride, rebelliousness, and genuine power of humanity was rebuffed by God.

Real towers have been built since antiquity—some of them truly impressive even by modern standards.

The Egyptian obelisk at Luxor, a pink-granite monolith that stands seventy-five feet high and weighs 230 tons, is more than 3,300 years old and commemorates the reigns of the pharaohs Ramses II and Ramses III. It was given to France as a gift by the viceroy of Egypt in 1829 and stands to this day in the Place de la Concorde in Paris.

The Ziggurat of Marduk/Etemenanki was a seven-tiered tower that stood 300 feet square and 300 feet high in the Babylon of the seventh century B.C., almost 3,000 years ago.

The Colossus of Rhodes was built on the island of Rhodes on the edge of the Aegean Sea about 300 B.C. It was a statue built of bronze on an iron frame that rose 110 feet high above a 50-foot base. It was one of the Seven Wonders of the Ancient World, and inspired the French sculptor Auguste Bartholdi to create the Statue of Liberty. The two statues are identical in height from toe to head, stand in the same attitude, and serve the same function in the harbors they respectively command.

The lighthouse of Alexandria was built about the same time as the Colossus, in the third century B.C. on the island of Pharos, just off the coast of Egypt near Alexandria. It was made of blocks of white stone and stood 440 feet high.

These are not the only examples of great towers in the ancient world, but we mention them here as examples because they are the most famous and best known to us.

In modern times, we have many building towers that exceed 1,000 feet in height and communication towers taller than 2,000 feet. Under development as we speak is a skyscraper in the United Arab Emirates that will be 2,313 feet tall when it is completed around 2008. A proposed solar chimney in New South Wales,

Australia, has been found to be feasible from an engineering standpoint and will be 3,218 feet tall if it is built. Skyscrapers as tall as 4,000 feet have been proposed, although none of them have passed the planning stage.

In the case of these enormous modern towers, their usefulness is questionable but the Freudian implications are unmistakable and unavoidable. The impulse and energy to build these extreme structures is sexual, phallic, but it is completely self-referential and therefore, in a sense, masturbatory. Perhaps this was true of the ancient towers as well. They are forms of ego incarnation, statements of achievement reaching as high as resources and technology permit. They redound to the glory of the communities that build them, proclaiming as always the wealth and power of the builders.

But many towers are more modest in size and have practical uses as well.

• They spread sound and light as bell towers and lighthouses.

• They increase communication distances—as lanterns and bonfires in ancient times, as radio and TV towers in modern times.

• They have been used as fortresses, prisons, storehouses, and chimneys and to perform experiments.

• There are clock towers, watchtowers, and towers that support power lines and drilling equipment.

• There are control towers at airports and harbors that guide planes and ships.

• There are "ivory towers" used for self-imposed isolation and uninterrupted work.

They are used, in short, to live in, watch, communicate, support, store, defend, imprison, isolate, and experiment.

The towers in tarot are no different in their uses and implications than the ones we have described. Look through your deck at this point and find all the cards that have towers in them. When you have done this, give to the towers in each card one or more of the uses or meanings we have discussed or others you have discovered for yourself.

Think about what you have learned of towers in this class and apply their lessons to your readings and also to your understanding of yourself. This is actually a difficult and subtle task, but if you do it well, you will be handsomely rewarded.

Towers of the Moon Journey

Let's end with a journey. It will be a tower experience, and it will make what you have learned more personal, more immediate, and more useful. Look through your deck and find The Moon card. Place it face up in front of you and put the rest of the deck aside.

Look at the picture in the card carefully. Examine its details and remember them, so that you can see the entire picture in your mind with your eyes closed.

When you are ready, close your eyes.

See the landscape of The Moon in all its detail. Remember everything.

Open your eyes and look at the card again. Did you miss anything?

Once again, memorize the picture in detail. In a little while you are going to enter that landscape and have an adventure there.

Now, close your eyes. Breathe and relax.

Surround yourself with darkness and rest.

Ahead of you in the darkness a light appears. Move toward it.

The light is the light of the moon in the landscape of The Moon, shining through the open doorway of the card. In a moment, you will step through the doorway and enter the landscape of The Moon. This will happen on your next breath.

Find yourself on the path that begins at the edge of the pool. Move along the path until you stand before the two towers. Although no entrance is immediately visible, there is a doorway somewhere in the base of each tower. Choose one tower and find the way inside.

Enter the tower and explore what you find within. Let whatever happens there happen. Experience and enjoy.

The time has come to return. Leave the tower and find your way back to the doorway by which you entered the landscape. Stand before it. In a moment, you will step through the doorway back into the restful darkness of your inner state. This will happen on your next breath.

Float in that darkness for awhile. Breathe and relax.

As you float, contemplate all that you have seen, heard, thought, and experienced about towers in this lesson.

It's time to return completely now. Become fully aware of your surroundings. Take a deep breath and, when you are ready, open your eyes but stay in a meditative state.

Spend the next few minutes writing down the high points of your experience and your contemplation.

ANGELS

Hello, and welcome to our class on angels in tarot. In a way, this lesson will be different than any we've done in this series before. Up to now, the subject has always been a symbol, an object in the real world to which we first give meaning and then internalize as a description of our own most significant selves. But this time, we go to realms and beings beyond the real world and beyond ourselves, although those realms and beings touch and influence our own. We'll need to ask questions that are difficult to answer and look inside ourselves to discover what we believe. And then we'll need to ground whatever we discover in tarot and its uses.

Let's begin, as we often do, with some questions. The subject of this class is angels, and that by itself produces the first question, which is: Do angels really exist? Do you or don't you believe in them? What, exactly, do you believe about them?

That sounds like three questions, but it's really only one looked at from different angles.

The second question is: What is an angel?

Even if you don't believe in them or think they really exist, someone else probably does, so what do you think angels are for them?

The third question is: How would you know an angel if you saw one?

It may well be that angels do exist, but not in reality, not in the real world, except possibly as occasional visitors. That brings us to the fourth question: If angels exist, but not in reality, where then? Is there a place or condition that truly exists but isn't real? How would that be possible?

Actually, the lesson of tarot, which we've been learning for some time now, is that it is not only possible but also necessary. The ultimate lesson of angels in tarot is that much exists and much happens beyond the scope of the real. In fact, the mystery of reality may well be the greatest of all mysteries and perhaps can only be fathomed in a context larger than itself. That is a big statement and may take awhile to consider.

Here's an interesting corollary to that statement: There's a difference between what is real and what is true. It is possible for something to be either one and not the other. Each is a separate context, and each context has its own laws that produce very different results. It may well be that angels exist in truth and not in reality and affect reality only in special circumstances. Or perhaps there are other relationships between the true and the real that angels may help to elucidate.

But whether real or true or both or neither, angels do have a time and a place in this world. They exist in religion, in magick, in philosophy, in art, in psychology, and in history. They were born with Judaism in the Middle East and entered the living streams of Christianity, Islam, and Hermeticism as well, where they reside to this day.

Angels make their first appearance in the Old Testament. There they are called *malachim*, which in Hebrew means "messengers." Three times they came, performed jobs they were given to do by God, and departed—all without any fanfare at all. Because of the Jewish prohibition against making images, they were not clearly described or physically represented. Up to the time of early Christianity, angels were simply divine energies with no independent existence. Only later, in the Talmud, in Midrash, and in Qabalah, did they begin to increase in number, acquire names and attributes, and appear as central or major figures in religious stories.

Angels evolved, as all things do, and underwent two major evolutionary developments. From the bare-bones mention of malachim in the Old Testament, they developed in the early centuries of the Christian era into named beings, with descriptions, attributes, and, to some extent, personalities. A single book, whose authorship is unknown, was largely responsible for this evolutionary leap. The book is the powerful and influential Book of Enoch, written sometime between 200 B.C. and A.D. 200.

Much of our popular angel lore comes from this book, in which is described the ascent of the prophet Enoch to heaven and what happened to him there. Enoch himself is transformed into Metatron, the highest angel in the hierarchy of angels, and seven of the best-known archangels are named and described, including the four that make their appearance in tarot.

The Book of Enoch is mentioned in the Zohar as the source of Qabalistic magick and was praised by the early Christian fathers as being of divine origin. It is also a source of ritual and knowledge for Freemasonry and is perhaps the ultimate root of all Western Ceremonial Magick. To be valued by so many traditions that are normally opposed to each other is an honor given to very few works.

A few hundred years later, angelology took another great leap forward in the form of the creation of hierarchies or orders of angels, a way to classify and organize angels that had begun to proliferate. The best known of these hierarchies was designed by Pseudo-Dionysus, probably a single pen name used by several anonymous authors of the fifth and sixth centuries, A.D. That hierarchy was an arrangement of nine choirs, or concentric circles, of angels surrounding God at the center. These choirs were arranged in three tiers of three, each more powerful and influential the closer they were to the center. These nine choirs, or circles, of angels are as follows:

1. Seraphim
2. Cherubim
3. Thrones
4. Dominions
5. Virtues
6. Powers
7. Principalities
8. Archangels
9. Angels

The first tier of three is composed of seraphim, cherubim, and thrones. They form the innermost or highest court of angels, the only ones who have direct contact with the divine center.

The middle tier includes dominions, virtues, and powers. They receive the divine word from the angels above them and pass it down to the lowest tier consisting of principalities, archangels, and angels, who carry out divine instructions and interact directly with humanity.

Each choir of angels is said to have its own duties and responsibilities.

Seraphim, as described in Midrash, were originally seen as fire-breathing dragons who inhabited the highest heavens. As angels they remain associated with fire, but the fire is the love of God that is the original force of creation. Seraphim are rarely if ever directly perceived by humans.

Cherubim are known as the ones who pray and the ones who know completely. They are divine record-keepers, the scribes of the Book of Life, and the guardians of the Tree of Knowledge in the Garden of Eden. They also drive the divine chariot.

Thrones are the divine chariot. Together, they create a moving throne on which the divine form is seated and on which the divine glory can be directly perceived by great souls.

Dominions are the governors who regulate the duties and activities of all the forces of both the angelic and natural universes.

Virtues are the angelic source of miracles and grace.

Powers are the forces of divine protection, warriors on guard against the dark beings that inhabit the heavens and the earth.

Principalities are the angels who watch over the destinies and activities of the tribes, cities, and nations of humanity.

Archangels are, first and foremost, the leaders of the armies of heaven against the powers of evil. They bring divine messages directly to the particular human beings for whom they are intended, such as patriarchs and prophets, and carry out major divine missions on earth. They are also responsible for the activities of guardian angels and they lead human souls to spiritual realization.

Angels are the most personal and intimate of angelic beings, the ones closest to humanity. They carry our prayers to heaven and help us directly where they can. There is at least one angel for every person, and there is said to be an angel for every star in the sky. The number of angels that are said to exist depends on the theologian or angelologist consulted. Generally, the number has ranged from millions to quadrillions. Suffice it to say that there are enough to go around.

In tarot, we are concerned with only the archangels Raphael, Gabriel, Michael, and Uriel. These are four of the seven archangels named in the Book of Enoch. And, as a group, these four have acted together in a number of biblical adventures.

Michael is the archangel we know best, and he appears in the lore of all three Western religions as well as in the rituals of Ceremonial Magick. He is the warrior who, in the Book of the Revelation of St. John the Divine, defeated and imprisoned Satan. He also guides willing souls on the path to divine illumination. His name means "He who is as God."

Gabriel is the archangel of prophecy, revelation, and resurrection. He guides souls from the realm of the spirit to embodiment in the womb and wakens them again from the slumber of physical death. It is Gabriel who tells Mary of the coming of Jesus and dictates the Koran to Mohammed. His name means "Mighty One of God."

Raphael is the healer, the reconciler and uniter of all things wounded, sick, broken, and dysfunctional. His name means "Healer of God."

Uriel is a messenger of both punishment and salvation, a force of fire and transformation. He is said to have warned Noah of the coming of the flood and to have punished Moses for his sin of omission. It is said that the angels gave Qabalah to humanity, and it was Uriel in particular who was charged with this task. It is Uriel who is said to guard the gates of Eden with his fiery sword. His name means "Light of God."

At this point, it might seem that we are ready to examine the role angels play in tarot. Almost, but not quite. Before we do that, we need to return to the discussion arising from the questions we asked at the beginning of class.

What is an angel? How would you know one if you saw one? Where, in what world or context, does an angel live? What purpose do angels serve in the structure of creation?

Here are some short, possible answers to these questions. They are only suggestions, since nothing definitive can be said, but you may find them useful and thought provoking.

1. What is an angel?

Originally, as we said before, they were mentioned rarely and only briefly described as divine messengers, without names or descriptions. They were extensions of God and not separate from their source. Over time, they became semi-autonomous energetic beings created out of divine names. They were capable of both error and rebellion and could cause problems as well as solve them. They could even be magically invoked to serve the purposes of a magician or called upon by individuals to help with their personal difficulties.

2. How would you know one if you saw one?

In another series of evolutionary steps, angels went from minimal verbal descriptions to visual representations in religious art as ethereal, vaguely male human forms, to modestly winged and robed but wonderfully built human forms without obvious gender but otherwise male in nature. This progressed to an inclusion of childlike and feminine forms, plus much more magnificent wings and halos. During the Renaissance, angel representation reached its peak with glorious color and form, which was slowly reduced to our present popular angel images of pretty women and children all dressed in white and having halos and swanlike white wings.

3. Where, or in what context, does an angel live?

Although each of us has our own feeling or intuition about this, the formal religious answer is that angels dwell in the seven or more heavens that exist between human beings and God. They may, and do, affect the real world and the real lives that are lived here, but they live elsewhere.

4. Why were angels created? What purpose do they serve in the scheme of things?

This is a question we didn't ask or discuss at the beginning of the lesson because it would have been premature. And the answer is not to be found explicitly stated in the literature of angelology. But the answer is fairly simple. Angels exist to carry out divine wishes, commands, and edicts. They are the executive bureaucracy of God.

An analogy might be useful here. Imagine the government of the country you live in, with its formal structure of leaders, lawmakers, judges, and any other special group needed to govern. Whatever is said, required, demanded, or mandated by that formal structure, will have no life or impact if things aren't actually done by someone. Every law and command has to be implemented—actually carried out. This is the function of bureaucracy on all levels, and it is the function of angels in the structure of creation. Angels get things done.

• • •

With these short answers to our questions in place, we can return to tarot and see what can be done with our four archangels—Raphael in The Lovers, Michael in Temperance, Uriel in The Devil, and Gabriel in Judgement—as well as those same angels in The Wheel of Fortune and The World. In these two cards Raphael (air) is the man in the upper left corner, Gabriel (water) is the eagle in the upper right corner, Michael (fire) is the lion in the lower right corner, and Uriel (earth) is the bull in the lower left corner.

When any of the archangels show up in a reading, if they catch and hold your attention, the first thing you can say with reasonable certainty is that they have a special message just for you. The

THE LOVERS.

JUDGEMENT.

WHEEL of FORTUNE

THE WORLD.

THE DEVIL.

TEMPERANCE.

second thing is that something is being done at the very moment about the issue in hand. Somewhere, somehow, forces are at work on the issue of the reading, and a resolution is probably near at hand. The kind of message and the kind of resolution depends on the nature of the angel.

It's time to test what we have discussed in an actual reading. First, ask yourself a question that really needs an answer. Write it down.

Angel Reading

Look at your question again. Make sure it asks exactly what you want to know. If it needs to be modified, do that now.

When your question is solid, choose a spread to answer it. You may use a spread you already know or you can create a new one.

Next, take out of your deck the six cards that contain visible angels— The Lovers, The Wheel of Fortune, Temperance, The Devil, Judgement, and The World. Shuffle them and choose one. Put this card face down in front of you. This will be one of the cards included in your spread.

Replace the remaining angel cards into the full deck, shuffle, and draw the rest of the cards you need.

Arrange all your chosen cards in the spread pattern. They can be all face up, or you can lay them out face down and turn them over one at a time.

Read the spread in answer to your question, paying particular attention to the angel card. The angel will have a special message for you, separate from and in addition to any other information you get from the spread. If another angel card turns up in your spread, that angel will have an additional message.

• • •

You remember that at the very beginning of this class we said that it would be different than any of the ones that preceded it. That's because angels are not symbols. They do not begin as commonly observable facts in the objective universe that we give meaning to and internalize. Instead, they originated with a few words of the Old Testament. From those words humanity has created and elaborated angels into what they have become. They begin as suggestion and then become real as inner experience turned into art, story, and anecdote.

Angel Experience

Before you are finished with this lesson, you should make the attempt to experience an angel, if you can, in order to make the angel real.

Close your eyes. Breathe and relax.

Surround yourself with darkness and rest there awhile.

In a moment, you will begin to look through the darkness of your own inner world for the place where angels live within you.

Begin to do this now.

Take your time. This place exists, and you can find it.

When the place of angels opens within you, enter it and fully experience whatever happens there. If you can't find it, or don't want to, experience your inner darkness as a rest from thought and activity.

The time has come to return.

Re-enter or remain in your inner darkness and float there for a moment.

Become aware of your actual surroundings.

Take two deep breaths and, when you are ready, open your eyes.

Welcome back!

TEMPLES

Hello, and welcome to our class on temples in tarot. With this lesson we reach the end of a path, and we will see where it has led. There are secrets here, as there have been all along, but the nature of a true secret is that even when you are standing in the midst of it, there is nothing to see.

Let us tell you the first secret of this class. There are no temples in tarot. Look through the deck. Find the cards that hint at a temple but do not show it. See if you can tell from these cards what the temple is like—either outside or within. What is there about these cards that says to you, "Here is a temple"?

What is a temple?

How do you know one when you see one?

Can a temple be known by any other kind of awareness than sight?

Formally, a temple is a building set aside for the worship of a deity. "Temple" is a generic word encompassing terms like "church," "synagogue," "mosque," and "grove." Within the temple there can generally be found a sanctuary where the deity of the place formally resides; a priesthood, complete with residence and inner chambers set aside for priestly offices; sacred implements, with places for both storage and public display; an altar, which can be any kind of ceremonial table or platform; and a sacred image or some physical token of the presence of deity. The temple will have a formal entrance and a place or space of assembly.

A temple can be either a permanent and dedicated structure, or a temporary place of worship set up and taken down as need arises but formal in its arrangement nonetheless. Even such a temporary or periodic temple will have its officiating priesthood, altar, sacred images and instruments, entrance, and assembly.

These identifying signs are present in temples everywhere, in every social setting, from the tribal to the cosmopolitan, from the primitive to the highly civilized. They will be found wherever human beings recognize divinity in the world and in themselves. Temples are everywhere, and they always have been.

But a temple is a secret and contains a mystery. If it does not, it is not a temple. The mystery it contains is easier to describe and seems easier to grasp than the secret that it is.

The mystery a temple contains is the presence of its resident deity. To enter a temple is to be in the presence of this mystery. To engage in the practices of the temple is to immerse yourself in mystery. If the immersion is deep enough, you may actually become the mystery yourself. Almost everyone has had all or part of this experience and will recognize the description of it.

But the secret a temple is will not yield to such a simple and recognizable description.

As numinous, purifying, and uplifting as temple mysteries can be, they are what they are and nothing more. Temples are here, and other things are there. An invisible but definite veil separates the sacred from the profane. That is precisely why temples exist. The special light they shed does not shine beyond their doors. Temples are built to be entered and also to be left.

Temples are physical. They are real places, given sanctity by the intention of their builders and by the sacred objects and ceremonies they contain. A physical temple is one mystery out of two. It is mysterious because no effort of the builders would make it so if deity did not choose to inhabit it.

This first mystery can be called the temple of stone. "Temple of stone" is a symbolic name that can be given to any physical structure built to serve its god.

In many, if not all, spiritual traditions, the human body is also said to be a temple. It, too, houses a divine spirit, and that spirit makes the body sacred in principle. But for the body to become a temple, it must be educated and dedicated to its sacred purpose. When that happens, everyone who comes in contact with it will know they are in a felt but unseen presence.

That is the second mystery of the temple, and it can be called the temple of flesh. Anyone who wishes to do so and acts to make it so can become a temple of flesh, a divine house. This is true regardless of the divinity the body houses. You can become a temple if you truly wish it.

In this second mystery, the separation between sacred interior and profane exterior becomes less clear. The person who is home to an awakened spirit looks like everyone else but shines with a permanent, though undefined, light. The world in the immediate vicinity of such a person seems somehow different and better than its usual self. When you find yourself in the presence of such a person, you will know it without necessarily knowing how you know, and you will be happy to be there.

The mysteries of these two temples are the felt but unseen deities that dwell within them. Without the indwelling divine presence, temples have no mystery at all. They become what everything else is, dead ordinary. Stone is just stone. Flesh is just flesh.

In these two mysteries, temples are only shells. Deity dives into them and disappears completely, leaving only a faint glow to remind you of its presence. That glow alone is enough to satisfy the need of most people for any divine presence whatever.

That glow is all the mystery that temples ever contain. But what, then, can be the secret of what a temple is?

A human being, you perhaps, can sometimes catch fire with the certainty that divinity can really be found, not just remembered. Then, like the princess who kisses the frog and releases the enchanted prince who has disappeared within it, your awakening gaze touches the world and its ordinariness disappears, leaving you face to face with your god. Then nothing is ordinary or ever will be again. The temple of stone and the temple of flesh no longer simply contain the divine presence. They are that presence.

You are that presence, and everything you see and touch becomes that presence. This is the secret of what a temple is. It is called the temple of spirit.

To accomplish such a feat of vision is a nifty trick if you can do it, and that's where tarot comes in. A temple is not a visual symbol contained in any of the cards. The whole of tarot is a temple. The glow of pure spirit is present within it. That is its attraction. Of course, people can't actually see it. Even its students and enthusiasts don't see it so much as sense it, just the way worshipers do in a church, a synagogue, or a mosque.

But when you know that tarot is a temple, built of symbols instead of brick or stone, you are halfway to becoming a temple of flesh as a reader. In your physical person, you can begin to shine with knowledge. The words you speak to a querent will be the right words. What you see in the cards will be true as well as accurate. All the symbols that make the structure of tarot—its names, numbers, and images—will speak through you, and you will become an oracle in truth.

With time, effort, and intent, it is possible to arrive at this oracular state, to contain it within you. But as extraordinary as this is, something even greater lies beyond it. That is the secret of becoming what speaks through you, of being what you see and say. Then you will go beyond knowing the mysteries of tarot—you will be that mystery.

The temple in tarot is the temple of tarot. All the things you have learned about tarot over time have been building blocks of that temple. In this way, learning tarot is like the process of initiation in Freemasonry and the magickal orders of the Hermetic tradition. It is a process of continuous enlightenment, and it binds its parts into a great and unsuspected unity.

Not an awful lot of people have seen the temple of tarot or even heard of it. It may be that you don't see it yet or even want to. But if you do, it can bring you to amazing knowledge and skill and transform your whole experience of life.

All that we said so far in this class may have lit a lamp for you, or it may well be just words, just talk. Before we finish, let's do something that will help to make the temple of tarot real.

Building the Temple of Tarot (Part 1)

In a moment, you will begin to consciously build the outermost shell of the temple with knowledge you already possess, at least in part. Read through all the following instructions before actually doing them.

First, mentally name each of the Major Arcana in order. As you do so, visualize each card's number and also the complete image of the card. If one or more of the Majors does not come to mind, go on to the next card you can remember.

When you are finished with the Majors, review each card of the Minor Arcana, including the court cards, mentally saying the number or name and suit of each and then seeing the image of the card as clearly as you can. Work through one suit at a time in any suit order you wish.

Take your time. Complete this task, if you can, in one sitting.

Close your eyes. Breathe and relax.

Begin.

When you can name and visualize every card in the deck, the build-ing stones of the temple of tarot will have arrived on site, ready for assembly.

INTEGRATION:
RIVERS, TOWERS, ANGELS, AND TEMPLES

Hello, and welcome to our integration class for rivers, towers, angels, and temples in tarot. These four symbols capture the essence of the Hermetic vision, which is contained in the saying, "As above, so below." It is the most famous of all sayings in the esoteric universe. If there is magic in tarot, if there is purity and spirit, it is distilled in those four words.

As above, so below—the whole of creation in a nutshell.

But a nutshell, though big enough, is also too small. Our four symbols give us everything it contains and more. In fact, when their sense is grasped, it tends to crack the nutshell wide open.

This lesson deals with what may be dangerous matters. It may shift the foundation of your most cherished perceptions. For Western magick, as well as for the three major Western religions, to many of whose assumptions most of us unwittingly subscribe, above and below is at the heart of everything. Spirit, divinity, God, one's purest self, lives high above and far away. The body, physical nature, ego, one's poorest and weakest self, lives below, right here.

The whole apparently circular journey of flesh and the spirit is the movement of spirit downward and matter upward, the reciprocal engine of emergence and return that we have talked about so often.

Rivers

But both emergence and return are the flow of spirit downward. This is the symbol of the river in tarot. The endless flow of spirit waters the garden of the world, fills it with goodness and wealth, and gives it life. To float on the current of the river is to be in harmony with the divine intention. To follow the whole course of the river to its apotheosis in the sea is to finish the journey of return without changing direction.

In tarot, rivers speak of harmony and effortlessness, of cleansing and enriching, of letting events evolve and unfold. Allowing them to reach their natural conclusion without fear and with a minimum of interference is a continuous act of faith.

Rivers catch and channel the endless falling rivulets of small events and minor dramas, carrying them all away as streaming karma and leaving the landscape clean.

The lesson of rivers in tarot is that troubles dissolve and problems resolve if you simply float upon the intent of the world.

Towers

As rivers move with gravity, towers struggle against it. As rivers flow from above to below, towers rise from below to above. Towers are expressions of effort. They are symbols of discontent.

For the builders of towers, what *is* is not enough. What *can be* is better. The future is better than past or present. Work, skill, talent, challenges met and overcome—these lead to improvement of self and world. Heaven is not a gift of grace; it is an earned achievement.

Towers rise. They point at distant goals. To conceive a tower is assume an obstacle, a problem, or a difficulty. To complete a tower is to win a victory over things as they are. Towers challenge entropy, the tendency of things to run downhill to an anticipated chaos.

In their highest sense, towers in tarot are the symbols of your ambition. They assume a faith in your own abilities and your willingness to work to create whatever you need. Their simple statement is that problems don't go away by themselves. They need to be dealt with. Their message is: Plan. Don't give up. Point at a goal, earn it, and it will be yours by right.

The tower is a prime symbol of success. Divinity is involved only as the source of the problem your tower is meant to overcome.

River is to tower as divine is to human, as flow is to effort, as nature is to artifice, as organism is to mechanism. This apparent disparity, however intense at its root, for the most part merges seamlessly in our everyday awareness into our everyday process. The energies of above and below together make us who we normally are and who we are normally conscious of being,

And that brings us to what we don't normally see and what we are not normally conscious of at all.

Angels

Angels are neither above nor below. They live and act in a world between. They neither rise nor fall, neither work nor flow by nature. They are the servants of both God and man, but they themselves are neither divine nor human. They never fail, nor do they achieve.

They never begin, nor do they arrive. They have neither goal nor direction, and so they are quite free of the issues of emergence and return, except to help with them.

An angel is somewhat like the elevator operator in a tall building. He has a job to do, but he is quite unconcerned with what floor you get off at or what you do there. And he has a life of his own. This is the key to understanding angels. They have lives of their own. And this opens the door to some tricky questions.

Do they? Do they have a separate existence? Do you exist separate from the divine source, and angels live separate from both?

There is an intuition, a suspicion, in us all that assembling our experience of being alive and present into a number of separate levels is not quite right. God up there, us down here, and angels in between. A simple arrangement, but perhaps a little clunky.

Angels in tarot serve to remind us that above and below by themselves are not a complete explanation. Two worlds are not enough. If there are two, they need at least a third to bring them together.

Angels exist to serve, but to serve they must be invoked. They must be called from either above or below, and when they are called, they must appear. That is their power in tarot.

Call an angel into a reading as you have learned to do, and it will appear. If an angel appears in a reading unbidden, it was sent. Angels are messengers of power. To call and receive messengers of power is an act of intense understanding, though to discuss the uses and responsibilities of angelic power is beyond the scope of this lesson. That such a power even exists is a secret, one of many contained in the imagery of the cards.

Temples

Is it a surprise that one of the greatest secrets of tarot is contained in a symbol that isn't even visible? The temple, last of the symbols in our series, is yet another whole world to add to above and below.

Within it is everything that exists—the three worlds of above, below, and between. That is its mystery. The temple's secret is that everything, all of it together, *is* the temple. The secret of the temple in tarot is that tarot, too, is the temple—every card, every meaning, and every use of it.

The secret of the temple transforms it, so that nothing in it is ordinary. You see that everything is made of numinous light. But that leads to a second secret, the biggest one we have seen and the most dangerous to grasp.

The temple's light is not sacred. The divine presence is not its source, since divinity itself is within the temple along with everything else. The light that illuminates the temple is the felt presence of the mystery that entirely surrounds it.

The temple of being, like everything in it, is a mystery. Mystery flows away from it endlessly in all directions—uncontainable, unexplainable, unappeasable, undiminishable.

Within is every explanation of mystery we can conceive. The temple walls are built of our explanations. They serve to protect us from the annihilating vastness of the unknowable. *Ain Soph*, the nothing without end that Qabalah names but can do nothing about, is an attempt to gingerly touch the unknowable with one uncertain finger.

The temple that contains us contains everything we can name. Tarot is a model of that temple. It is constructed of the great explanations of spirituality, psychology, magick, and culture. No matter how heavy or cumbersome the explanation, tarot has been able to carry it and make it light.

When you do a tarot reading, be aware, if you can, that you are manipulating a mystery of many parts. You and your querent alike are mysteries, as is any issue that concerns you. Be aware, if you can, of your true stature, and let your readings be filled with light.

We are at the end. Nothing more can be said that would be useful. But before we go . . .

Close your eyes. Breathe and relax.	*Living*
	Darkness
Surround yourself with darkness. Take the time to make the darkness complete, and then rest within it.	*Reading*

Become conscious of the darkness as alive and aware. Find the pulse of your own awareness within the darkness. Be slow and thorough.

The darkness is now complete, and it includes you.

Nothing separates you from it.

There is no difference between above and below.

Here is the same as there.

Now is the same as later.

Inside is not different from outside.

You are a living darkness.

Experience this fully.

In a moment, you will open your eyes and see the world, but you will stay in a meditative state. The living darkness will remain with you, fully aware within your awareness.

Take two deep breaths and, when you are ready, open your eyes.

Stay in a meditative state and keep the mystery of the living darkness with you.

Clear your deck if you know how. Then shuffle it, and as you shuffle, let a question arise from within. Wait for it—don't force it.

When you are ready, lay out a spread to answer your question.

Read with the secret knowledge of the mystery that surrounds you and illuminates the cards from within.

SYMBOL SPREAD:
RIVER, TOWER, ANGEL, AND TEMPLE

This spread is based upon the symbols studied in our last set of classes: rivers, towers, angels, and temples. The reading can be done either without a question or with "What do I need to know, learn, understand, or do about . . . ?"

There are two parts to this reading: preparation and the reading itself.

As you may recall, although there are hints of sacred space throughout the deck, there are no temples per se to be seen. The deck itself is the temple. We are about to take that idea one step further and teach you how to personalize the temple of your deck. Once you have learned how, you may, if you wish, perform this preparatory ritual before any reading session.

Preparation: Building Your Temple (Part II)

1. Find all the Major Arcana cards and lay them out in order from 0 to 21.

2. When you have done this, gather them together in an ordered stack. Begin by placing The World face up in front of you. Put the other Majors face up, one at a time, on top of The World in reverse order, ending with The Fool on top. Then turn the entire stack face down and put it to the side.

3. Do the same for each of the four Minor Arcana suits, ordering them from king to ace.

4. Place the four kings face up. Then place the other cards of each suit on top of the kings in reverse order. When you are finished, you should have four separate piles with the aces on top. Keep all four piles face up.

5. Arrange the stacks of Minor Arcana cards into your Elemental Array. To do this, look at the four aces and decide which you like best at this time. Place this pile to your left.

6. Continue to choose the aces in order of preference, placing each subsequent pile to the right of the previous one.

7. When you are finished, you should have four separate stacks showing the aces in your order of preference from most to least liked, with the pile of Major Arcana cards off to one side. Here is an example:

1: Majors   2: Wands*   3: Cups   3: Pentacles   4: Swords**

*most liked   **least liked

8. Look through the Major Arcana cards and find your birth cards, if you know them. Remove them and place them face up on the table. (If you do not know your birth cards, that's okay. Follow the directions without them.)

You have gathered together the building blocks of your temple. Now it is time to complete the structure. Keep the sacredness of your act in mind as you perform these final steps.

9. Turn each stack face down, leaving them in position. Keep your birth cards face up.

10. Gather the separate piles of cards together into a single stack with the Majors on top (excluding your birth cards), followed by each of the four suits in your order of preference. Your least-liked suit will be at the bottom of the deck.

11. Take your birth card with the lower number and place it face down on the top of the deck and place the card with the higher number at the bottom. If your birth cards are Sun-Wheel-Magician, insert the Wheel of Fortune card towards the center of the deck.

12. Hold your completed temple between your hands as you breathe and relax. If you like to offer a prayer before beginning a reading, this is an excellent time to do so.

The Reading

It is now time to proceed with your reading. If you would like to use one of the four questions mentioned earlier (What do I need to know, learn, understand, or do about . . .), concentrate on it while thoroughly shuffling the deck. If not, focus on being in a receptive state.

Note: If you are reading for someone else and have first created a personal temple of your deck, briefly shuffle the cards before handing them to your querent to shuffle more thoroughly.

The layout consists of four cards:

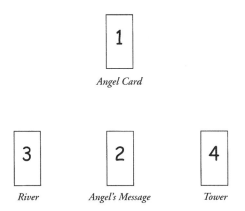

ANGEL CARD

1. The Archangel who has been sent to deliver your message.

To find out which angel has been sent, shuffle your deck and then turn the cards over one at a time until one of the following cards appears:

- *The Lovers:* Raphael is the healer, the reconciler, and uniter of all things wounded, sick, broken, and dysfunctional. He is the angel of love and joy.

- *Temperance:* Michael is the leader of the divine armies against the forces of darkness. He is the angel of wrath who brings justice, offers protection, and guides willing souls on the path to divine illumination.

- *The Devil:* Uriel is a force of fire and transformation. He illuminates situations and gives warnings. He is the angel of laughter and secrets.

- *Judgement:* Gabriel is the bringer of prophecies and revelations. He is the angel who resurrects what has died and awakens what is asleep.

The Angel card gives you the context of the reading. If you have asked a question, consider how the nature of the angel who has appeared addresses that question.

Place the Angel card in position #1 at the top.

Choose the next three cards in the deck directly following the Angel card and place them in position according to the layout diagram. Use any method you like to interpret them.

THE ANGEL'S MESSAGE

2. The message you need to hear right now.

This card contains a message of importance or the primary answer to the question you have asked.

RIVER

3. What flows easily.

The River card describes the type of energy that will carry you along naturally, with little or no help or interference from you.

TOWER

4. What requires your effort.

This card describes what is demanded of you in the way of effort, attitude, or resources.

• • •

This is a powerful spread that consciously invokes angelic energy. Use it with care. It is best to allow some time to contemplate the message you receive.

AFTERWORD

As a young man I was introduced to tarot as an adjunct to my study of Rosicrucianism and the Hermetic Qabalah. (The latter is a facet of the Hebrew Kabbalah embraced and utilized by students of magick and the Western mystery traditions.) It was never my intention to use the cards as a divinatory tool, an activity frowned upon by the mystery school I was attending through a correspondence course. Indeed, I was counseled that if I were to use the cards to tell fortunes it would cripple me spiritually. I took my teachers at their word and proceeded for the next three years to use the cards for meditation purposes only.

Part of the school's curriculum was the requirement that each student paint his or her own deck of tarot trumps. The course provided an unpainted deck of the twenty-two trumps bearing clean black outlines of the figures on each card and very strict coloring instructions. Each card took two weeks to color during which time certain texts and meditations were assigned. I must admit that at the end of forty-four weeks I knew every detail of the cards.

The mystical power inherent in the images was apparent from the first weeks of my study. The evening I completed coloring The Fool would become one of the most memorable of nights of my life. During the night, I experienced the most marvelous vision. It was unlike anything I had ever experienced (even in the sixties!). It was so intense that even after I woke up and turned on the light, the living images continued to play across the screen of my vision.

I won't bore you with the curiously personal details of this nocturnal initiation. It is enough to say that it *was* an initiation—not an initiation into the bricks and mortar order that mailed me my monographs each week, but into the temple of tarot itself. I knew without a shadow of doubt that my two weeks with The Fool card had reprogrammed my psyche and triggered a glimpse of a higher lever of consciousness. What would become of me when I finished the whole deck? I thought.

Now, over thirty years later, tarot continues to play a central role in my life. It is my constant companion. Its perfect Qabalistic structure and construction is a constant source of wonder and illumination. It is the spyglass, counselor, and commentator of an examined life, and I view the streaming events of my ever-changing existence as the shuffling, spreading, and reshuffling of the cards. My relationship with the cards has long ago transcended the stage of, "Oh my! The damned Prince of Cups is beating me with the 3 of Disks again." The cards have ceased to be metaphoric cartoons of my intellect and reasoning process, and have literally become communicating angels of my intuitional life. In the language of tarot I am moving from the world of Swords to the world of Cups, and tarot gives me the secret language to do so, the vocabulary to voice such ineffable spiritual subtleties. That is perhaps tarot's greatest gift to the student of the soul—the ability to communicate with the various parts of our being, to give form and meaning to parts of our psyche that are formless and indefinable. The secret language. The gift of the god Thoth.

I've long since abandoned my eschewing of tarot as a divinatory tool. This is not to say that I consider my readings for other people to be a form of fortunetelling. Tarot, or indeed any oracle, cannot show us the future or directly answer our questions. Tarot is simply a vehicle for perfection, and eternal truth is revealed in perfection. Used with proper attention such oracles serve to announce the status not of the future, but of the *Great Now*. It's the person who consults the oracle who must somehow glimpse the future or hear the answer to his or her question in that announcement.

That being said, I can honestly say that I have never consciously made an important decision based upon information I've received from a tarot reading (especially my own) or any other form of divination. This is not because I don't have confidence in the wisdom and efficacy of oracles, but because I am a self-centered, self-involved, bullheaded old fool who seldom takes wise advice from any of his friends or family, let alone from a pack of cards or the roll of the dice.

I *have*, however, encountered adepts whose tarot insights are eminently worthy of decision-making counsel. Two of them, in fact, are the authors of this book for which I am proud to pen this brief afterword. The Amberstones are dear friends (I officiated at their wedding) and directors of one of the most respected tarot schools in the world. Their tarot credentials are impeccable, but their greatest qualification for speaking with authority on this sacred subject is the fact they comfortably embody in their lives a conspicuous level of balance, wisdom, and sanity. In short, they are walking examples of lives illuminated through contact and mastery of the secret *language of tarot*.

—Lon Milo DuQuette
Costa Mesa, California

EXERCISES *and* SPREADS

CHAPTER SEVEN: RIVERS, TOWERS, ANGELS, TEMPLES

INDEX

ABOUT *the* AUTHORS

Ruth Ann & Wald Amberstone are cofounders of The Tarot School. Together they teach, write, and publish about tarot on all levels from divination to psychology to esotericism and magical practice. They were each awarded the honorary rank of Certified Tarot Grandmaster in 1998. More than a thousand students have taken live classes at The Tarot School since it opened its doors in 1995. Hundreds more from around the country have participated in Tarot Telecourses (an innovative program of classes given on the telephone), and students from all over the world have purchased recordings from The Tarot School Audio Course Series and study *The Tarot School Correspondence Course*. *Tarot Tips*, The Tarot School's e-mail newsletter, has thousands of subscribers worldwide. They are the authors of *Tarot Tips: 78 Practical Techniques to Enhance Your Tarot Reading Skills*.

The Amberstones have taught numerous workshops at tarot conferences nationwide, as well as producing continuously successful tarot events of their own. The New York Tarot Festival, presented in June 2002 by Ruth Ann, Wald, and the students of The Tarot School, was the first international tarot symposium to be held on the East Coast. The Readers Studio, also produced by The Tarot School, is an annual tarot conference providing cutting-edge practical techniques to intermediate and advanced students, professional readers, teachers, and authors.

They can be found on the Web at *www.tarotschool.com*.